WABI-SABI WISDOM

Inspiration for an Authentic Life

ANDREA JACQUES

KYOSEI
PRESS
vancouver

Published by Kyosei Press, an imprint of
Kyosei Consulting International, Inc., Vancouver.

Kyosei Press
Suite 502, 2045 Barclay Street
Vancouver, BC
Canada
V6G1L6
www.kyoseipress.com

Kyosei Press can bring Andrea Jacques to your live event. For more information, please contact Kyosei Press at 1-855-459-6374 or visit: www.kyoseiconsulting.com/services/speaking/

Cover design by Natasha Johnson and Boyan Blocka
Cover photograph courtesy of Morty Bachar (www.lakesidepottery.com)
Edited by Joshua Grant

ISBN 978-1-988267-01-2
ISBN 978-1-988267-00-5 (ebook)

First Edition

For my friend Lori-Ann, who kicked my butt to get this book out into the world; my husband Boyan, whose passion for perfection inspires me to reach for the stars; and my son Zen, who shows me daily that I am loved and beautiful exactly as I am.

CONTENTS

Acknowledgments

My deepest thanks go out to my team at Kyosei Consulting (Boyan Blocka, Joshua Grant, and Natasha Johnson), who got behind me when I set a crazy deadline to publish a book in 26 days. Their editing, graphic design, and whip-cracking were instrumental in making it all happen.

I would also like to thank my mom, Darlene, for being ready to jump in to look after our son at a moment's notice when the demands of writing, work and life just couldn't be made to fit together as seamlessly as I would have liked.

To Joy Saison, I owe a huge debt of gratitude for the opportunity (and deadlines) of writing for Tokyo Families Magazine for the last five years.

A special thanks to Morty Bachar of Lakeside Pottery Studio (www.lakesidepottery.com) for graciously allowing me to use a photo of his beautiful kintsugi pottery for the cover. Not only is his art amazing, he is a living example of the *kyosei* spirit and the path of the *shokunin*.

Last but not least, I am grateful to my husband, Boyan, for the inspiration for the cover of the book, his original version of the "I'll have mine with Wabi-Sabi" chapter, and his unending patience in looking after our home and child while I sequestered myself in my office during early mornings, evenings and weekends to edit 100,000+ words down to what finally made the book.

Preface

This book might not exist were it not for my good friend, Lori-Ann Keenan. The quality that I most admire about Lori-Ann is the unapologetic authenticity that fuels her ability to "get shit done." When she decides to do something, she just does it. She doesn't censor or judge herself. She doesn't care what others think (and if she does, she doesn't let it stop her from doing what she wants and being who she is). She knows who she is, follows her heart, and doesn't waste a ton of time trying to live up to any standards other than her own.

One night over dinner, we were talking about her latest project — a book she is writing on the lessons she has learned in her life - and the topic of editing came up. She told me that many people were offering to support her in writing her book by volunteering to edit it, but, in typical Lori-Ann fashion, she had politely declined their offers. When I asked why, she replied, "This book is about my stories and lessons. I want to tell them with my words, my grammar and my spelling mistakes. I am good with publishing it as it is. I want it to be authentically me."

For me, this struck a deep chord — of shame. For more than a decade I had dreamed of writing a book. I had at least five books that were in various states of completion, but somehow I had let life (and others' opinions of my work) get in the way of taking even one of them all of the way to the finish line.

As Lori-Ann has known me for this same decade, she is well-acquainted with my author aspirations — and my excuses. When she saw my dawning realization that I too could just put my work out in the world without getting bogged down in doing things the "right" way, she threw down a challenge: finish a book — any book — and publish it by the end of the month.

With a mixture of fear, excitement and determination, I accepted her challenge.

That was January 5th, 2016 and, if you look at the date on the copyright page of this book, it was published as an e-book (and posted, for the world to see, on Amazon) on January 31st, 2016 — just 26 days later.

On the walk home from that dinner, my mind was spinning. Which of the many books I had underway could I complete? Which one *should* I complete? Recognizing a pattern of getting caught in inaction, I decided to pursue three angles and see which flowed best.

I had first drafts of two books complete, but I was stuck. I knew I needed outside feedback before I could push them through to completion. The next day, I sent each one to a different friend with an explanation of the challenge I had set for myself, and the one-week deadline I had for their feedback.

Not wanting to waste a whole week doing nothing, I started thinking about other projects I could move forward to ensure I met my goal. Almost immediately the idea for this book surfaced. For more than a decade I had been writing articles on life, work, well-being and achieving soulful success for various magazines. It dawned on me that I might just have enough of these writings to pull together into a book.

I was shocked to discover that, in ten years, I had published more than 100,000 words in three different magazines both locally and internationally. As I skimmed through my articles, I was further surprised to find myself thinking, "these are pretty good." Not perfect, mind you, but good enough.

In that instant, a title and a concept sprang into my mind — wabi-sabi.

Wabi-sabi is a Japanese design aesthetic and worldview that places value on the transient, unfinished and imperfect nature of life. It sees beauty in the rough edges of both people and things. It is at peace with what is. It values all that is real and authentic, finding joy and fulfillment in the good, bad and ugly rather than longing for unattainable fantasies of the ideal.

In keeping with the spirit of wabi-sabi, this book is imperfect, unfinished and, above all, authentic.

It is most definitely imperfect. The chapters are of different lengths. A compilation of articles published over a period of more than ten years, the voice with which I write is inconsistent. I suspect that I both contradict and repeat myself - possibly even in the same chapter. My Japanese is terrible, so it is likely that at least some of the kanji selected for the beginning of each chapter are wrong.

It feels unfinished. Even as I wrote these words — the final ones in preparation for turning it over to my team to begin the process of publishing it as an e-book — my perfectionist self wanted to pull it away from them. I wanted to delay another week, another year, forever, until I could add one more thing that would surely make it better.

Above all, however, it is, authentic. That is, in fact, the whole point. I took it on to challenge myself to face my fears and put my work, and myself, out there in the world just as I am. The definitions at the beginning of each chapter represent an unofficial, but hopefully useful, take on concepts central to deepening your ability to live an authentic life. The thoughts I offer in each chapter are intended less as a "how to" guide, and more as a sharing of the struggles, insights and learning that I've encountered as I have lived, gained wisdom and found my unique path in life.

In the final days of completing the manuscript, we needed to decide on an image for the cover. I had been playing with dozens of sub-titles, but none of them felt quite right until my husband reminded me of *kintsukuroi*, the Japanese art of repairing broken pottery with gold.

Having studied tea ceremony when I lived in Japan, I knew this was the perfect image to use on the cover. Wabi-sabi is an integral part of Japanese tea ceremony. Each ceremony contains rituals for tea drinkers to stop and admire the unique beauty of each chawan (tea bowl). In my lessons, I had been taught to admire the imperfections in the glaze, color and shape that made each chawan uniquely beautiful.

The kintsukuroi technique is an extension of this. In tea ceremony, tea bowls that break or crack are not simply discarded. They are repaired, often using a combination of lacquer and gold. These cracks of gold then become part of the beauty of the object, drawing attention to the breakage and repair as something to be appreciated rather than disguised or discarded.

This is an inspiring metaphor for living life more fully. We have all been broken and built ourselves anew. Rather than seeing our mental and physical scars as things we must hide, it is time that we learn to appreciate and even celebrate the things that make us wise, beautiful and valuable. Our cracks of gold.

It is my hope that, in some small way, each person who reads this book will find a measure of gold to help repair their broken places. That by embracing their wabi-sabi perfection they will, as I have, learn to better appreciate their authentic beauty and find the courage to give their gifts to the world.

Andrea Jacques — January 2016

WABI-SABI WISDOM

Inspiration for an Authentic Life

I'll Have Mine With Wabi-Sabi

Wabi-sabi

The art of appreciating the beauty of the unfinished, imperfect and impermanent in yourself, your life and the world.

In Western society, we obsess about perfection. The perfect mate. The perfect car. The perfect job. Perfect looks. The perfect life. It never ends. As a collective we sand-down the rough edges of reality until there is no substance left. At what point do we evaporate into a forgettable mist of uniformity?

Enter *wabi-sabi.*

Put simply, *wabi-sabi* is the Japanese idea that true beauty exists only in the imperfect, impermanent and incomplete. From an aesthetic viewpoint, its characteristics include asymmetry, uneven roughness, simplicity, economy, modesty and austerity.

When one admires the large stones "floating" in the otherwise perfectly manicured sands of a zen garden, one experiences *wabi-sabi.* When one enjoys tea from a rustic, irregularly handcrafted tea bowl, one tastes *wabi-sabi*. When one sees a picture of Marilyn Monroe's face — flawless, save for that one beauty mark on her left cheek — one sees *wabi-sabi*. It's that thing "not quite right" that somehow brings it all together in a unique, beautiful experience greater than the sum of the parts.

But *wabi-sabi* speaks to something much more profound and fundamental than aesthetics. It gives insight into the wisdom of nature and the creative power at the core of life.

Throughout nature, not only can imperfection be part of unique beauty of something, it often also *spurs* the very existence of the system to begin with.

When scientists began modeling the evolution of learning with mathematical models called neural networks, they discovered that homogeneity lead nowhere across generations. In short, a system that is too perfect eventually collapses. It lacks the resilience and evolutionary building blocks to withstand uncertainty.

Introduce a random stress, however, and magic (specifically, learning) happens. As scary as it might feel, when we introduce (or allow for) imperfection, systems evolve — and flourish.

Wabi-sabi is the grain of sand that irritates the oyster to create the pearl, the conditions that make every snowflake unique and the discontent that drives the maverick techno-evangelist to push the world to "think different." New businesses and industries are formed to address an economic imperfection. Remove the imperfection, no business.

In reality, then, everything we know and all that we are is the product of *wabi-sabi*. The perfection of nature is found only in it's imperfection. There is no evolution without adversity. Instead of trying to eliminate our imperfections or alienate individuals courageous enough to be different, it's high time we acknowledge — and even celebrate — them as a key variable in the mathematics of our survival.

Perhaps, more importantly, it is time to stop focusing only on survival, for this is where the deeply ingrained fear of our imperfection and our brokenness comes from. We fear being different lest we be cast out from our tribe, unable to survive on our own. We fear showing weakness lest someone else see this as a sign that they can eat us for dinner.

If we give into this fear of being real, different and vulnerable, however, much of what makes life worth living ceases to exist. Love, art, friendship and invention — all of these depend on having the courage to be authentic, take risks, fail and pick ourselves up to try again.

The pages that follow are an invitation to you to step beyond surviving and contemplate what it means — and what it takes — to truly thrive in your life and work.

The chapters do not need to be read in any particular order. Look at the table of contents, pick any chapter title that calls to you and start there. Jump around. Read and re-read again. Notice how your relationship to the words and yourself, changes. Last but not least, give yourself permission to see the beauty of all that you are and find the courage to share it with the world.

ONE

Lessons from a Florist

Happiness
(Kōfuku)

The blissful state that emerges when you focus on wanting what you have instead of having what you want.

I studied *ikebana* — Japanese flower arranging — for some time while I was in Japan. At one point, I was practicing for up to 20 hours per week. I was not the best student, but my continued practice over the years has brought me great joy. It has also sparked a great deal of insight from extrapolating its principles to my life and work. The following is a distillation of some of *ikebana*'s key principles which I hope will prove useful for bringing more beauty to your life as well.

1. Less is More

Despite my teacher's wonderful instruction, the *ikebana* principle that most challenged me was the idea that less is more. Each lesson, she gave me a bunch of flowers, instructed me on the principle to apply that day, then let me loose to create my masterpiece. She sat there quietly as I started out, nodding her head in approval or making minor adjustments. As I progressed, I would notice her starting to frown. She kept quiet and didn't stop me as, despite her teaching on the importance of simplicity, I proceeded to use every single flower she had given me. I couldn't help myself. They were all so beautiful. It felt wasteful to not fit as many as I could into my arrangement.

While many of my flower arrangements still tend towards excess, I think that my teacher would be pleased to know that I have at least learned to apply this principle in my life.

The moment I knew I had arrived occurred just a few months ago when our good friends, 20-year veterans of living in Japan, came to stay at our place while we were out of town on holidays. On our return they couldn't stop raving about how much they had loved staying in our apartment because it was so "zen", uncluttered and peaceful. They wanted to know how we kept it that way, but I was at a loss to explain.

For several days, their question echoed in my head. I knew our space hadn't always been this way, but over the years, despite having a child, we had managed to reduce rather than increase our clutter. Several days later it hit me. My previous need to keep every thing of beauty or usefulness in my space — the same need that made me need to use ALL the flowers — had disappeared. Somewhere along the way, I had learned to let go of those things (and people) that, while beautiful, served mainly to distract me from enjoying the beauty that was naturally present in space, silence and time to be alone. I had learned to understand, and love, enoughness.

This principle has now become an integral part of my coaching practice. I love seeing my clients discover their state of enoughness, and experience the energy and freedom it brings.

To begin discovering your place of enoughness, consider the following:

- What do you have in your space that you rarely or never use?
- How much of your stuff do you really love?
- How much of it brings you joy?
- How much of it are you holding onto because of fear?
- How might all this stuff be distracting you from being present and creating new experiences?
- How might it be keeping you stuck in the past?

Give gratitude for the value all these things and people have added to your life. Then let them go.

I find it much easier to let go of both things and people when I remember this: holding onto a good thing does me more harm than good if it is not *my* good thing.

2. You Don't Need Symmetry for Balance

Like nature, *ikebana* is asymmetric but balanced. Life is like this too. When I coach my clients around their desire for more balance in their lives, I challenge them to consider whether they need more balance or more passion, more relaxation or more meaningful challenges, more vacations or more time for deep introspection. The beauty, and the balance, come from understanding that in nature there will always be strong and weak, yin and yang, dark and light. The more we strive for perfection and try to eliminate what we perceive as the negative side, the more likely we are to cheat ourselves of the opportunities for greater harmony that are present in the opposing forces of our lives and work.

When you understand this, you might begin to question whether bringing balance to your life might involve working more (but on the right things), instead of working less.

My retired clients are an example of this. They come to me because they have grown bored with their new "balanced" lifestyle. It has time for a bit of everything, but no driving force on which to focus. Everything in equal parts is not always a good thing. Each individual needs to find their own asymmetry to create the balance of activities and people that is right for them.

3. Let Nature Be Your Guide

In creating an *ikebana* arrangement, the true art of the practice emerges from learning to connect with both your own nature and the nature of the elements you are arranging. The goal is to determine what is already there and bring it out, rather than deciding what you want to create in advance.

To apply this principle, I encourage my clients to ask themselves "What is wanting to happen (or not happen) in my life?" and then to adjust their path accordingly.

Western sensibilities tend to favor making plans and sticking to them as essential to a life well-lived. *Ikebana* teaches us that the path to a beautiful life is more easily found when we flow with what is — both inside and outside of ourselves — instead of trying to sculpt something out of sheer will. This doesn't mean giving up on your goals. It means understanding that, just as every year has its seasons, every life, relationship and goal has its seasons as well. When you do this, you can give yourself permission to lean in to the phase that you are in, embrace its beauty, and do the work that season is calling you to do.

4. The Container is an Element of the Creation

In *ikebana*, the container dictates the type of arrangement. While there are general trends that tall thin containers have different arrangements than long flat ones, the unique colors, shapes and sizes of each container are meant to serve as both the inspiration and the foundation for the creation.

In the same way, each of us is born with our own unique container. You must design your life and work to suit the nature of your container. This is not just about the way you look on the outside and the physical capabilities you have; it is also about the shape and nature of your insides. Don't waste energy wishing that your container was different. Embrace what you have been given and begin to create, knowing that, with mindfulness, awareness and patience, a beautiful life can be built from any foundation.

Perhaps one of the things that I love most about this art form is that, despite its simplicity, there is endless variety in how the principles can be applied to produce a stunning result. As in life, however, your power to create not only beauty but happiness rests on your ability to see the truth of all that is both inside and around you — and express it in a way that is uniquely you.

TWO

Creative Living

Evolution
(Shinka)

*The creative living process that evolves you
into your highest and best self.*

Many people long for more from their lives, yet few take advantage of the multitude of opportunities around them to create it. This topic came up over coffee with some fellow entrepreneurs one day when I lived in Tokyo. We had all started out teaching English, but our enjoyment of that work lagged very quickly, and we had all cultivated businesses based on our passions. Why, we questioned, had we made this leap when so many of our colleagues had stuck with teaching English despite the same decreasing fulfillment? After a far-ranging conversation that spanned several hours, we agreed that the common element was not some superhuman intelligence we possessed, but our capacity for "creative living."

That conversation was more than two decades ago. My work as a career and business coach has since given me many opportunities to witness the power this mindset has to help people bypass mediocrity in their lives and work and move on to their customized version of the big leagues. My work has also helped me to understand that cultivating our capacity for creative living is really about learning to embrace, rather than resist, our deep-seated need to constantly create and evolve.

In Japanese, *shinka* is the word most commonly used to express the concept of evolution. *Shinka* can also be translated as progress, real worth, true value and apotheosis. Defined as "the perfect form or example of something" and "the highest or best part of something", the apotheosis translation gives insight into the true goal of creative living — evolving into the perfect example of our best selves. Taken together with the other translations, *shinka* offers us the wisdom that creative living requires evolving in ways that create true value and represent progress for both ourselves and, ideally, for the world. Simply stated, creative living involves making the most of available resources to evolve into an expression of the best of who you are.

You don't have to be an artist to live creatively, but you do need to understand (and embrace!) the following five stages of the evolutionary process:

Chaos

Are you experiencing chaos, confusion, dissatisfaction or uncertainty in any area of your life? Fabulous! You are entering the creative process.

The archetype of the tortured artist whose creativity comes out of her angst is an accurate representation of this stage. Chaos is a catalyst for creativity. It is the signal that it is time for change. Things are shifting. You are entering into a new cycle of growth. Your old image, values, beliefs, and attitudes no longer fit. That job that you used to love just doesn't excite you anymore. All your co-workers are incompetent, your boss is an imbecile, and everyone expects you to pick up the pieces. Or worse, despite knowing you have every reason to be happy, you can't shake the nagging feeling that something is missing.

Heed the signals. Trust your instincts. Face your fears and prepare to let go.

Introspection

Chaos will naturally lead to the next phase: introspection. This involves an increased need for silence and space. All artists recognize this as essential to the creative process. Our society often refers to it as "down" time, a reflection of the high value we place on activity as the foundation of personal worth. This belief is incredibly toxic in your quest for creative living.

Silence is vital. Turn inward, liberate yourself from old expectations of who you "should" be and discover who you are. For most of us, separating what we want from the expectations that our families and societies have for us is a monumental task.

Living in Japan for five years gave me first hand experience with the beneficial effects that separating from your nearest and dearest can have on your ability to listen to your inner voice. It removed me from all of the social rules I took for granted, forced a reassessment of my old assumptions and

necessitated learning to accept, or at least work with, an
entirely new set of values and beliefs.

Fortunately, moving to a distant land is not the only way
to gain this perspective. You can accomplish the same at
home by hanging out with different types of people than you
normally would, paying attention to the things you do simply
to please others or to avoid "rocking the boat," and making
a conscious effort to assess your values. As you get to know
your inner truth, independent of your needs for approval and
acceptance from others, you will begin to make choices that
are more in alignment with the highest version of yourself.
This ability to know and follow your inner direction is the
foundation of creative living.

Experimentation

The next phase of creative living requires action. It is time to
begin exploring and expressing these new ideas of who you
are and what you want. If you realize that you don't enjoy
teaching, figure out how to do less of it so you have time to do
more of something else. Take up a new hobby that excites you,
even if you think you lack the talent to be any good. The key
in this stage is to collect as many different experiences and as
much knowledge as you can about anything that interests or
intrigues you.

In the experimentation phase, creative living artists are
constantly challenging their beliefs and perceptions. They
look for new ways to view and benefit from their current
circumstances, even if the circumstances seem limiting in the
moment. This sparks new ways of viewing themselves and the

world, and keeps them open to opportunities to evolve into their best self.

Asking questions will help you to remain vigilant to unwanted beliefs and expectations that will sabotage your evolution. Try on new perspectives and get unstuck by asking:

- What if everything I thought was right was wrong?
- What would happen if I combined A and B?
- How can I do more of A and still have time / money for B?
- What if I did the opposite of what I think I should do?
- What if I had to start all over again without any experience?
- What is another way I could accomplish that same thing?
- What would I do if I wouldn't feel (guilty, dumb, embarrassed, selfish, egotistical, etc.) about it? These negative feelings are often based on judgments - either your judgments of yourself or the judgment you have experienced from others when you have expressed what you wanted to do in the past. Challenge those feelings and the beliefs they are based on. Examine the long term consequences of holding on vs. letting go.

Synthesis

Watch. Listen. Feel. Pay attention. Notice the insights. The synthesis phase is about tuning in to the opportunities that appear for you to express, create and learn in just the ways you desire. Stay open. These opportunities often appear in unexpected ways. Don't be impatient. Trust that you will evolve toward a deeper understanding of how to express your unique life path at a speed ideally suited to your needs,

Expression & Flow

As you become more aware of who you are and what you want, you will develop the inner strength and conviction to express yourself creatively through all of your choices. To stay in the flow, creative living artists constantly cultivate a liking for the periods of chaos that signal growth and change. They learn to build silence and introspection into their lives. They use their passion for ongoing self-discovery to break away from set roles, methods and standard. Above all, they honor their need to create and contribute to the world through expressing who they are.

A commitment to creative living is the most effective career strategy I have seen for realizing both success and overall life fulfillment. Remember, however, that creative living, like any other natural process, is cyclical. Your experiences, with all of their challenges and discoveries, will continually return you to the beginning of the cycle and prompt you to evolve so that your life more accurately expresses who you are. Ultimately, when the joy of being in the creative process becomes one and the same with that which you are creating, you will have found the never-ending source of fulfillment you have been seeking. And you will realize that it was inside of you all along.

THREE

Turning Crisis Into Calling

Crisis
(Kiki)

*Something you attract when you aren't listening
to what your heart is calling you to do.*

I was just twenty when I had my first "midlife" crisis. I was halfway through a degree in psychology and was working part-time as the assistant director of the student crisis line at my university. Theoretically, I should have loved this job, but the reality was different.

Sitting in the call office one afternoon, covering for a volunteer who was sick, I realized that I dreaded the thought of having to answer a call. This was not a new feeling. I really loved managing the volunteers, but for months I had ignored the fact that I hated dealing with crisis calls from students who had serious psychological issues. Suddenly it dawned on me: this presented a pretty significant challenge for my intended career as a psychologist! Just like that, the whole career path I had laid out for myself crumbled. I found myself at loose ends wondering what to do next.

Poring over job possibilities in the student career placement center one afternoon, I chanced upon a job posting for teaching university students how to find jobs. Despite little experience in finding jobs myself — and even less experience teaching — I managed to land the job.

To my great relief, I discovered that I loved working with *these* students. They were highly motivated and just needed a little guidance to discover their career direction. This crisis taught me I was more suited to work with people who needed help to go from good to great than those who needed support to go from crisis to coping.

My second career crisis came at twenty-three while working as the career development director of a health care union. It was an amazing job that involved delivering career development and employee engagement training for health care workers. While these types of initiatives are, thankfully, becoming more mainstream in organizations today, twenty years ago this was very pioneering stuff — especially coming from a union.

It had taken me two years to get these programs up and running and we were finally ready to roll them out on a larger scale. Unfortunately, the leadership — and hence the organization's priorities — changed. When budget time came around, my departments budget and all our jobs were cut.

Getting laid-off came as a complete shock. I was hurt, angry and scared about my next steps. After the initial shock wore off, I looked back on what I had accomplished. It occurred to me that I had essentially built a separate business within the organization. I knew it wouldn't be nearly as easy to get started on my own, but this crisis, along with a healthy dose of naive optimism, led me to become an entrepreneur.

Two years later, a third crisis started to form. Something wasn't quite right.

On the work front, I loved my business doing career development training, but I felt torn. My students wanted to turn the negative experience of being injured into an opportunity to find more meaningful work. They didn't want to take just any job. This desire was at odds with the interests of the companies who hired me. Their main goal was to minimize costs by returning these people to work as soon as possible.

On the personal front. I was engaged to be married in three months. As I was preparing to send out wedding invitations, I couldn't shake the nagging feeling that I was making a mistake. When I had taken the union job six years earlier, I had postponed my dream of backpacking across Asia on my own. Getting married would mean the end of that dream. I knew I could still do it with my husband after we were married, but the more I thought about it, the clearer it became to me that an essential element of my travel dream was doing it on my own.

I also started to think about the fact that I had never experienced what it was like to live alone. I was living with my fiancé at the time and, prior to that, had always had roommates. I worried that I would end up stuck in an unfulfilled marriage but be scared to leave because I was afraid of being on my own.

To complicate things further, while I was grappling with all of these thoughts I received an unexpected opportunity in the form of a job offer. A prestigious international outplacement company offered me a junior partnership. This was a very lucrative offer and a great honor to receive at my age. My friends and family all told me that I would be crazy to turn it down.

So there I was with a great life, a great job opportunity and a great guy who wanted to marry me. I should have been excited, but I wasn't. My gut was telling me that if I accepted the job I would be "sucked into the corporate world" and never return to my dream of being an entrepreneur. I didn't want to look back on my life and have regrets, but calling off my wedding and shutting down my business to put on a backpack and traipse off to Asia on my own seemed like a pretty big leap. I spent many sleepless nights trying to convince myself that all of these thoughts were just normal pre-wedding jitters.

While all of these things scared me, I also believe strongly that fear is the flip side of passion. This third crisis put that belief to the ultimate test. I knew that if I didn't act on what my heart was saying I would always wonder what could have been.

I turned down the job, called off the wedding, shut down my business, sold my car, gave up my apartment, put my belongings in storage and set off to travel Asia for six months with nothing but a backpack.

I had no idea at the time that answering that call to travel would be so pivotal in finding my calling. That choice led to the five years I spent living in Japan, during which I began to develop the systems I now use for helping people and organizations create meaningful work, and healthy, high-performance cultures.

This crisis also taught me that crisis, no matter what age it occurs at, is less a crisis than it is a calling.

Your crises call you to listen to your heart, discover your passions and align with your purpose. You get these calls throughout your life — intuitions, gut feelings and other messages that are trying to guide you towards meaningful work, vibrant health, sustainable success and a fulfilling life. When you don't act on these messages, the calls become more insistent in mid-life. They can generate health, career, or relationship crises and become more and more difficult to ignore.

Whether you are in the middle of a crisis now (mid-life or otherwise) or simply wanting to prevent one, take the time to explore the messages you have been ignoring. Ask yourself what your heart has been trying to tell you. What is it that you would really love to do, if only circumstances were different? If you look back, what "calls" have you been consistently ignoring?

It takes courage to listen to these messages from your heart — and even more courage to act on them. But listen. The payoff is worth it, and the price of not listening is high.

FOUR

The Flow of Achievement

Achievement
(Seika)

Something that gets easier as you learn when to apply force and when to step into the flow.

To succeed in the adult world, we learn how to push, plan, set goals, strategize and work hard. These concrete skills teach us that there is a direct link between cause and effect — if you do x, then y will be the result. While this approach does get results, it has two downsides:

1. you start to believe that you can always control results; and

2. the nose-to-the-grindstone achievement approach inevitably morphs hard work into being the goal itself, ultimately leading you to lose sight of what the hard work is for.

Fortunately there is another aspect to the process of creation that, once mastered, brings success and fulfillment along with achievement: your capacity to cultivate faith and embrace flow.

Soulful success requires you to have faith in yourself and your dreams while also understanding that you can't control everything through plans and strategies. It asks you to develop the courage to have dreams despite knowing they might not turn out exactly how (or when) you want them to. It requires the faith that what you get when you step into the flow is always better than what you thought you wanted to begin with. It requires, in the words of St. Francis, "the serenity to accept the things you cannot change, the courage to change the things you can, and the wisdom to know the difference."

One of the things I love about traditional Japanese art forms such as *chado* (tea ceremony) and *ikebana* (flower arranging) is their understanding that mastery has two stages:

1. learning concrete skills and knowledge; and

2. developing the ability to apply them in a way that adapts perfectly to the circumstance.

Diagrams of the shapes that can be used to arrange flowers in *ikebana* and rules about the number of times to turn the tea bowl represent the easiest and most concrete level of learning. True mastery does not emerge, however, until you know these basic skills so thoroughly that you can disengage your mind and adapt the application of your knowledge to the moment and the environment.

There is similar duality in the Japanese martial art *aikido*. You need to learn the basic moves (punching, blocking, etc.), but once learned, the next level of mastery does not involve learning to punch harder. It involves learning how to use the energy of what is happening around you in service of the objectives of winning the battle. This involves understanding when punching or blocking *is not* required at all. In the same way, mastering the ability to achieve requires cultivating the following four skill sets:

Master the Basics of Achieving

Goal-setting, planning, organizing, prioritizing, focusing, and creating systems are the basic building blocks of success. If you don't have these skills, invest the time to learn them. You needn't look far for help. A quick Google search will turn up a multitude of books and other resources on these topics. Once you learn them, make it a habit to use them. It is not how much you know but how much of that knowledge you use that matters most.

Align With Your True Nature

If the goals you are striving for and the strategies you are using are based on "shoulds," forcing yourself to achieve them will eventually lead to burn out. To sustain your ability to achieve your goals over the long term, it is essential to become more aware of your unique values, strengths and passions, and only set goals that are aligned with them. If the targets you set for yourself are not intrinsically compelling, you will lack the fuel and focus required to see you through the challenges of achieving them.

Slow Down to Pay Attention

Tapping into the flow of achievement requires that you learn to watch, listen and wait. Waiting makes successful type-A people nervous. They mistakenly see it as doing nothing, but this couldn't be further from the truth. Important work is being done in this waiting period. It is only in this space of waiting that you are free to do the work of noticing the messages, synchronicities, and coincidences pointing you in the direction of what is wanting to happen. When you move too fast and are focused only on where you are going, you miss the information and opportunities available in the moment to help you get there faster, more easily and in ways that are more fulfilling to your personal nature.

Cultivate Allowing

This is the hardest part. Allowing is tied up in our sense of our own worthiness. Most people find it much easier to feel they deserve something when they have worked for it. Allowing is not about sitting around and waiting for things to happen. It is about listening to yourself long enough to get clear about what you really want and paying attention to the signs of where the energy of the situation is trying to flow. From this place of clarity, it is easier and more productive to take action. Allowing is not about being passive. It is about actively re-engaging with the energies of the moment to determine right action. This means loosening your grip on your plan and staying open and attentive to how the universe is supporting you to live your purpose.

The real joy on the journey to achievement and success comes from embracing its duality. You must at once learn the skills and develop your artistry to apply them. If you do this, you will come to see success not as something to be achieved and endured, but as an adventure to be savored.

FIVE

Busting Busyness

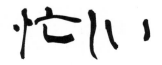

Busy
(Isogashī)
The art of distracting yourself from what really matters.

Does this conversation sound familiar?

"How are you?"

"So busy! I've been doing x, y and z. Time is flying. But that's what you have to do to get ahead these days."

"Yeah, I know. I've been really busy too doing a, b and c. I'm pretty stressed but it's okay because the money is great."

People wear busy like a badge of honor. Being busy makes us feel important, useful and relevant. There is some truth behind these feelings. Being busy can fuel your energy and performance — if you are busy with the right activities. Unfortunately, the need to feel important, useful and relevant is more likely to keep you busy in ways that drain you, causing you to fall further behind while fueling the vicious cycle of overwork.

One of my favorite clients, Mark (not his real name), has been going through this realization recently. In his twenties with tons of energy and passion for everything he did, Mark had his dream job, was growing his dream business on the side and was getting ready to go back to school to take the next step towards his dream career. He was definitely busy!

Mark and I worked together for several months on tools and techniques to clarify his priorities, increase his focus and manage people and projects more effectively. He did incredibly well applying everything I taught him, and was more productive than ever, but just as busy.

One weekend, he went away and had the chance to not be so busy. He took this as an opportunity to think deeply about the projects he cared most about, and to move those forward even though they did not feel as urgent as other projects on his plate. By the end of the weekend, he felt more energized, happy and peaceful than he had in ages.

When he returned to his regular full life the following week, he realized that there were large portions of his job that were not as fulfilling to him as the projects he had worked on over the weekend. He saw how much this work was draining his energy and, consequently, the time and energy he had left to work on the areas that would take him towards his long-term dreams.

Despite the prestige of his job, the lure of a stable salary and the fear of "burning bridges" in the organization he worked for, Mark determined that he needed to quit his job and make a move to focus on growing his business. True to his personal style, Mark wasted no time in taking action on his insights.

Contrary to his fears, support for his decisions and opportunities to do more of what he loved poured in. He soon felt energized and excited about his work again, but realized that he could easily lose this if he became too busy. To prevent this, we worked to establish clear guidelines around how many hours he wanted to spend in various types of activities each week, and restructured his product and service offering, as well as his pricing, to ensure that he can meet his financial goals within the hours he had identified.

People who are chronically busy justify their addiction by telling themselves that things will slow down soon. The reality though, is that life won't slow down — unless you make it.

The first step is to acknowledge that being busy meets your ego needs for feeling valued and important. Recognize that constantly seeking an external validation "fix" is just like any other addiction. It has harmful effects long term. Your addiction to external validation distracts you from finding the healthier sources of validation that can only come from within.

Chronic busyness is also a great way to keep yourself from discovering and pursuing what it is you really want to do. It keeps you safe from the risk of doing what matters most — and the possibility of failing at it. The irony of not prioritizing time to pursue your dreams is that, while you are guaranteed not to fail, you are also guaranteed not to achieve them.

Trying to cram the most important stuff in without letting anything else go doesn't work either. You need time and space to fuel the creativity that will breathe life into your dreams (and yourself).

Make time soon to stop and take stock.

- Are all of the things you are so busy with truly energizing and fulfilling for you? If more than 50% of your activities are not fueling you, you are headed for burnout.
- Now look at your list and decide which ones you are going to let go. Yes, there are all kinds of reasons why you can't or shouldn't, but each activity that does not fuel you in some way is draining you.

Above all remember: good-busy is filled with excitement and leaves you feeling tired but satisfied at the end of the day. Bad-busy is heavy with stress and leaves you feeling exhausted before the day has even begun. Ultimately, it's up to you. Good-busy or bad-busy — you choose.

SIX

Soulful Success

Soul
(Tamashī)

Something that it is easy to lose on the road to success.

The biggest challenge with achieving success lies in its definition. The assumption is that when you have the good job, the house, the car, the husband or wife, the 2.5 kids, the healthy retirement savings account, the nice clothes and the vacations, you have succeeded. The unfortunate reality is that many people who have all of these things still feel unsuccessful. The whole concept of having a midlife crisis is a testament to this.

There are two definitions of success in the dictionary. The first, *the attainment of wealth, favor,* or *eminence,* is what most people believe that they are striving for. The challenge with defining success this way is that it is based on external comparisons. When you define success like this, you are bound to feel forever lacking. There will always be someone who has more wealth, respect or fame than you.

The second definition, *a favorable or desired outcome,* is more promising. It gives us deeper insight into the nature of success, and why it is so elusive. If success is about achieving a favorable or desired outcome, doesn't it follow that you must first be clear on the outcome you desire? Here is where the difficulty starts. How much money equates to wealth? What constitutes respect and how much is enough? At what point are you considered "eminent"? More importantly, why do you even want "success" to begin with?

The answer to this is at the heart of why people who are successful in worldly terms still feel unsuccessful. They have failed to achieve their desired outcome. Why? Because what they really wanted was not the wealth or status they worked so hard for. It was the feelings of happiness, ease, confidence or fulfillment that they assumed would come with it.

In order to find soulful success — success on your own terms — you need to take a step back and determine your real desired outcome. This can be hard to do when surrounded by all of the trappings of consumer society that paints a pretty consistent picture of what success *should* look like.

One of the biggest blessings of the time I spent living in Japan was that it gave me the opportunity to be a misfit. I was clearly not Japanese, so I didn't feel the pressure to fit in with their cultural rules and expectations. I was also far from home, so I no longer felt the pressure to fit in with my own culture's definitions of success. This allowed me the freedom to experiment with new ways of doing and being, reinvent myself on a daily basis (if I felt like it) and entertain new ideas of what a successful and fulfilling life would look like for me. Through this journey, I came to understand that success is something each of us must define individually, and that external, material measures are but one small part of the equation.

The first step in achieving success on your own terms is to define your target clearly. This starts with finding a new term — soulful success — to use when referring to what you are working towards. Soulful Success is the state of vitality, abundance, confidence and contentment that results when you trust in your ability to achieve goals that are intrinsically meaningful to you. Soulful success does not necessarily mean that you have "arrived" in the traditional sense. It is characterized by the desire to continue growing, learning, achieving and actualizing your potential in ways that are *personally fulfilling,* regardless of whether these achievements are recognized or valued by others.

The following six P's are key markers of soulful success:

Passion

You are doing something that you love. Ideally this is part of what you are paid for, but it should not be limited to your career. Soulful success is characterized by the ability to follow your passions both inside and outside of work.

Purpose

You know why you are here and how you make a difference. Your work and life have purpose beyond just making money. You know that your life and work make the world a better place in ways that are meaningful to you, even if they are not recognized as significant by others.

Prosperity

You experience genuine prosperity because you have defined your state of "enoughness." You understand that the pursuit of money for its own sake can create scarcity rather than abundance. You understand how much money you need to live according to your values and passions and resist the temptation to live outside of your means. This does not preclude you from aspiring to increase your financial abundance — if that is what you desire. It simply means that your sense of prosperity is not determined solely by your income.

Potential

You understand that fame and wealth are poor measures of whether or not you are fulfilling your potential as they force you to compare and compete with others. Not everyone who fulfills their potential gets external fame and recognition. The brilliant computer programmer who pushes the boundaries of her abilities is fulfilling her potential as much as (and possibly more than) the famous entrepreneur who lucked into the right business idea at the right time. The key to fulfilling your potential is to constantly challenge yourself to grow, learn and break out of your comfort zone.

Present

Soulful success requires cultivating the capacity to stay in the moment and be grateful for all that you have instead of always longing for more. Many of the people who are most successful in worldly terms are consumed by feelings of inadequacy. They are driven into overwork and overwhelm because they cannot be content with the accomplishments and abundance they already have.

Process

Above all, achieving soulful success requires the ability to embrace success as an ongoing process, not a destination that can be reached. Contrary to popular belief, research shows that true fulfillment comes in the striving for something, not in its realization. The more that you can come to understand that, when it comes to success, the journey truly is the goal, the more likely you are to experience the fulfillment and happiness you are longing for in the pursuit of material achievement.

Take some time to step back and redefine success on your own terms. Use the above mindsets as guidelines for areas where you can begin to make mental shifts that will support soulful success — the space where internal fulfillment meets external accomplishment.

SEVEN

Ikigai and Aging Well

(Ikigai)
*That which gives value and meaning to your life. The
reason you are excited to get out of bed in the morning.*

Japan, like many countries in the developed world, is experiencing a marked increase in the percentage of its population that is over fifty. With this changing demographic comes an increased interest regarding what it takes to not only live longer, but to live better. One of the most comprehensive research projects in this area has been led by Dan Buettner's Blue Zones group. Based on data gathered from the five parts of the world where people both live longest and stay healthiest as they age, their research isolated nine key factors that contributed to aging well.

One of the key factors linked to increased longevity and wellbeing in these five "blue zones" was the Japanese concept of *ikigai*. *Ikigai* translates to life plus value, or that which makes life worth living. In English, this term is often translated as having a sense of purpose, but the Japanese concept of *ikigai* is much broader than this.

For some, *ikigai* centers on what they are most interested in giving or how they most enjoy making a difference. For a grandmother it might be helping out with their grandchildren. For a retired professor it could be continuing to contribute to research in her field. A businessman might find purpose and fulfillment by continuing to mentor his successor even after he retires. To discover what type of giving will make your life feel valuable and worthwhile, ask yourself the following:

- Who do I most enjoy helping? What do I most enjoy helping them with?
- What would I like to be remembered for? What legacy would I like to leave in the minds and hearts of my friends, family, community or industry?

For others, *ikigai* might center more on what they are most energized by doing. Whether it be driving, fishing, dancing, golfing, teaching, cleaning or solving math problems, a person who knows that their *ikigai* lies in doing certain things will do these things even if they do not get paid for them, or after they have formally retired. In fact, the healthiest people with the strongest sense of well-being have a difficult time relating to the concept of retirement. They simply plan to continue doing what they love to do as long as they are able. The answers to the following questions will provide some clues to this part of your *ikigai*:

- What kinds of task energize me the most at work?
- What activities energize me the most at home?
- What do I love learning, reading or talking about?
- What do I love doing so much that I would do it for free?

For still others, *ikigai* stems from how they most love being. It does not matter as much what they are doing as it does that they are able to be how they want to be while they are doing it. Whether they revel in being adventurous, analytical, whimsical, wacky, introspective, intense, intellectual or eccentric, they derive joy and energy from expressing their unique personality in everything they do.

This one can be a bit more difficult to define as some people feel that they have many different sides they want to express. While people do have multi-faceted personalities, certain sides of their personality may have been created because they were conditioned to think they had to be that way in order to be successful, liked, or fit in. One of the most challenging and rewarding aspects of the coaching work I do is helping people to separate which aspects of their "being" are their authentic selves, and which are simply manifestations of their need to be seen as competent and likable.

Here are a few questions to begin separating who you feel you *should* be from your true passion for being:

- What are the messages I received growing up about how I should be? Which of these feel like a "have to"? Which of these feel aligned with who I truly am and how I really want to be?
- What is my natural style? How do I like to do things? Am I slow and steady or fast and furious? Am I quiet or social? Observe how you are being when you are feeling most "at home" with yourself, and when you are feeling most like an impostor. Make note of the differences and consider how you might achieve the results you desire in ways that are more aligned with your authentic style of being.

The final element of *ikigai* that a person might focus on is what they are most excited about achieving or creating. From knitting a sweater to building their own cottage or working to end world hunger, these people are most energized by working towards their tangible vision of what they want to create. Regardless of whether their goals are large or small, this clear endpoint both focuses and energizes these people and gives them a reason to get up and go to "work" each day.

- What tangible results would you be most excited to achieve? This might include running a marathon, starting a business, renovating your house, teaching yourself or others how to do something, traveling, reaching a certain status in your career, or any other tangible goal. It doesn't need to be big. It just needs to be big enough to keep you focused, excited and geared up to take action towards it each and every day.

- What goals do you keep setting for yourself but never seem to take action on? Examine these more closely to see what they are based on. If they are based on what others have said you "should" want, or on what you think you have to achieve in order to get where you really want to go, you might want to stop and re-evaluate. An example of this would be thinking you need a PhD to get to the next level in your career. While this is sometimes true, many of my clients who thought they needed additional education to get where they wanted to go, found alternate paths when they got clearer on the end destination and accepted that they had no desire to go back to school.

Research in Japan has shown that a lack of *ikigai* is related with poor general health, increased risk of intellectual dysfunction and increased mortality in older people. Similar research in the West has also demonstrated significant health benefits for people of all ages related to having a sense of purpose and meaning. East or west, it is clear that discovering your *ikigai* is a crucial foundation not only for aging well, but for living well at any age.

But be warned: acquiring this personal sense of what leads to a meaningful life is not something that you can just flip the switch on once you retire. The more years a person spends disconnected from that which brings them the greatest sense of joy, aliveness and fulfillment, the more difficult it will be to reconnect with it and begin to make it part of their everyday life as they age. What's more, the connection with the things that make life feel worthwhile is a key source of energy and wellbeing. It insulates against stress and disease and acts as a buffer against the inevitable challenges that life throws your way at any age.

The bottom line: don't worry if you don't already know what gets you fired up to get out of bed in the morning — make it your *ikigai* to find out!

EIGHT

The Year of No Excuses

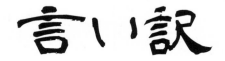

Excuses
(Iiwake)

*The ways you give yourself permission to let fear
stop you from being who you are meant to be.*

As each new year or birthday approaches, people make resolutions and set goals regarding how they are going to improve themselves and their lives in the coming year. Unfortunately, within a few months — or even weeks — most goal-setters fall off the wagon. Many have good excuses for doing so and tell themselves they'll get on with it tomorrow. In some cases, "tomorrow" stays only a day away for years!

Then there are those who claim that they don't believe in resolutions and don't make them. Don't be fooled. All of those slightly smug "I don't make resolutions" people aren't really so enlightened. They're just tired of letting themselves down year after year. Instead, they've decided that the best way to preserve their self-esteem is to stop setting goals altogether and simply try to be happy with whatever they achieve by default.

I know this because, by four years after the birth of my son, I had become a not so proud member of this second group. Despite several years of resolutions to lose the last 10 pregnancy pounds, finish one of the three books that I had almost completed before he was born, and exercise more, it felt like I had accomplished nothing that I had set out to do. My excuse for my lack of follow through, I realized, was that I was tired. Incredibly tired.

The first year after my son was born, I gave myself permission to not write, or exercise, or do anything that wasn't an absolute necessity. Between running my business and getting used to the whole motherhood thing, this was a pretty reasonable way of reducing my stress and preserving my sanity. I promised myself that I would get back in the groove when my son was sleeping through the night. But the second year came, and the third and the fourth and I was still exhausted. Despite the fact that he was sleeping fine, there never seemed to be enough time — or enough energy — left over to do anything else.

Late in 2012, something shifted. I was mucking around online seeking inspiration for my next magazine column when I came across the phrase *moushiwake gozaimasen*. In Japanese, this is similar to "my apologies," but it literally means "there is no excuse." As I read over the phrase and poked around for its meaning, I had an epiphany of accountability. I clearly understood that being tired was simply an excuse. Likewise, I saw that I had the power to make no excuse acceptable for not doing what I wanted to do. Strangely, as I saw this power of choice, I was able to forgive myself for not seeing these excuses for what they were — fear — and for letting them stop me.

Next, I asked myself, "What do I want badly enough to stop making excuses? Where do I most need and want to set a goal and commit to achieving it?" One clear answer emerged. I was tired of being tired. All of the other things I wanted to do depended on me getting my old levels of energy back. I was not prepared to use being tired as an excuse anymore. I decided that this year I was making only one resolution: to get my groove back.

Then, a funny thought occurred to me. Maybe there was actually a legitimate physical reason I was tired! This may sound painfully obvious, but my pre-baby self had always lived from the "there is no excuse" mindset. Because of this, I believed that being tired was all in my head. I thought I was just being lazy and needed to get a bit more sleep and exercise or needed to push myself harder. This assumption, I realized, further drained my energy. By facing this excuse head on, I opened myself up to the possibility that there was another reason I was tired. What if it wasn't all in my head?

Sure enough, a bit of blood work uncovered a few things that had gone wacky in my body chemistry, not the least of which was a very low iron level. Within a month, the iron supplements the doctor prescribed had already had a huge impact. My "too tired" excuse didn't go away overnight, but this small success gave me hope that I could get out of my slump. This hope — and the iron supplements — slowly started to restore the energy I needed to stay committed to making other small changes.

In my situation, it turned out that my excuse had some physical legitimacy. The reality, however, is that all excuses do.

That is why they are so powerful. The older we get the better we are at finding legitimate excuses for avoiding the things that scare us, and for putting off the pursuit of the things that would make our hearts sing.

It wasn't until I got curious about where I was stopping at incomplete that I was able to see a pattern in my excuses. Once I saw this pattern, I was able to evaluate a path to eliminate the excuse. While the first step on this path involved seeing a doctor, I was half expecting to find nothing physical to back up my tired excuse. If this had been the case I would have proceeded to whatever next step I could think of to get my energy levels back up to where I wanted them to be.

If you want to stop living on excuses and take back your power to live the life you really want, follow these steps:

1. Identify the areas where you keep stopping at incomplete.
2. List all of the excuses you use to justify stopping. Are there patterns? Is there one excuse at the root of them all?
3. Forgive yourself for letting excuses get in the way of doing what you really want to do.
4. Get clear on what you want badly enough to stop making excuses. Let go of anything else.
5. Decide what you need to do to eliminate the excuses that stop you once and for all.
6. Make a plan to achieve your goal and stick to it — no matter what.

Yes, I can hear you saying, "yeah but — ". My response to you is simple. Remember, there is no excuse.

NINE

Love and Other Drugs

Love
(Ai)

The addictive elixir that draws you to the people and pastimes with the power to bring you fully alive.

Love is an integral part of life. We crave it. We fear it. We need it. We resist it. Love is like drugs. There are many different types of love, and each type gives us a different "high," comes with different side effects and requires mindfulness to be used responsibly.

Romantic, erotic or sexual love is the first thing that comes to mind when we think of love. Because of its physical nature, this type of love is the most addictive. Being near the object of one's desires sends all kinds of juicy neurotransmitters coursing through our brains. Being away from those we love creates a bittersweet longing that becomes sweeter or more bitter depending on whether said object has gone away for the weekend or decided to dump you for someone else. As great as the highs are with this kind of love, the biggest risk is that these highs keep you focused on the other person at the risk of neglecting yourself.

A prerequisite for healthy romantic love then, is a healthy heaping of self-love. I'm not talking about narcissism, which creates an artificial high based on an overly inflated sense of your own worth and abilities. Healthy self-love — also known as self-esteem — gives you a different kind of high. If we were to equate it with food, healthy self-esteem gives you the kind of high you get from eating a huge plate of veggies. Erotic love's high is more like drinking a can of Coke, having a coffee or downing an energy drink. The latter "drugs" are okay in moderation, but without a consistent diet of veggies to balance it out, they provide no lasting sustenance.

Next comes unconditional love, which is usually equated with the parent-child relationship. The reality of love in this context, however, is often far from unconditional. The growing field of counseling and psychotherapy is a testament to the very conditional love that many people receive from their parents. The Japanese word for this type of love, *amae* or "indulgent dependence," is a far more accurate description of the kind of love between parents and children (and sets a far more realistic expectation of parents).

Unconditional love is an ideal to be aspired to by both the giver and the receiver, as it gives different but equal highs to each. For the receiver, there is a sense of safety, security and comfort that comes from knowing that they will be loved no matter how big of a screw-up they might be at times. For the giver, in those difficult moments where they are able to truly offer love without conditions, there is the high that comes from rising above one's baser needs, desires, fears and foibles to be able to be the "rock" for someone else.

Unlike the high of romantic love, the fix you get from practicing unconditional love lasts much longer. Giving it becomes addictive in a good way — just like eating your self-love veggies. Receiving it builds a healthy "backbone," and the mental and spiritual strength to stand up for what you believe in and follow your passions regardless of what others may think.

My favorite type of love — *ikigai* — is not an official type of love in many people's books. *Ikigai* translates as "something one lives for." I like to think of *ikigai* metaphorically as "the love of one's hands," like the love a master craftsman expresses through their passion, patience and dedication to create a finished product. While not everyone produces a physical product with their work, we all have the capacity (and the deep longing) to perfect our craft. Whether that craft is making objects, evolving ideas, or developing people, we all have a natural desire to discover and do work that we love.

The great thing about this kind of love is that the high a person gets from finding and expressing their *ikigai* does not depend on any outside participation. Lovers of control and independence often dig this idea so much that they veer off the path of passionate mastery and onto the path of the obsessive workaholic.

According to Freud, the foundation of our health and humanness can be seen in our capacity "to love and to work." Without the grounding force that the work we love provides, romantic relationships can pull us away from our true center. Without the other types of love, however, love of work can easily turn to obsession. Unconditional love is great, but does a disservice to both parties when it fails to set boundaries, or starts to enable in ways that prevent people from stepping out of their comfort zones to reach their full potential.

Fortunately, unlike with drugs, the secret to a great life lies in developing your capacity to imbibe regularly of all varieties of love. The perfect mix will vary for each person and change depending on their stage of life. Best of all, when used responsibly, the side effects of love are all good.

TEN

Harmony Without Compromise

Harmony
(Wa)

Blending the elements of life and work so artfully that the whole is more vibrant than any individual part.

Wa is a concept integral to understanding the roots of Japanese culture. Most often translated as "harmony," the everyday practice of *wa* in Japanese society centers around maintaining peace, unity and conformity within the group.

On many levels, the results of this cultural value are impressive. Despite having more than four times the population of Canada living in an area one twentieth the size, the Japanese manage to function with relatively little conflict. Unfortunately, part of this ability to function harmoniously is the result of a strongly ingrained social and business hierarchy that suppresses personal interests in favor of group interests.

The Japanese are not alone in this. Eastern and Western cultures alike achieve harmony (or at least the semblance of it) by subverting conflict, dissent and original thinking in favor of conforming to the status quo. It is important to note, however, that we as individuals are not blameless victims. We willingly sacrifice pieces of ourselves for conformity-based harmony because, at some level, it feels easier, safer or is more comfortable than rocking the boat.

Thankfully, there is another path to harmony that can avail us of the benefits without the downside.

In Japanese, *wa* also reads as "gentleness of spirit." In English, the definitions of harmony include "a pleasing or congruent arrangement of parts," "internal calm" and "an interweaving of different accounts into a single narrative." This kind of harmony is about creating a whole that is truly greater than the sum of the parts, not the result of disowning parts of yourself.

The following are some of the keys to developing this type of harmony:

Value All Voices

Recognize the many different voices (both within and without) and understand that each voice matters. In an a capella group, all voices have a unique part to play in creating the music. No single voice is more important than any other. When done well, it is almost impossible to tell who is doing what. The whole becomes greater than the sum of its parts, but each part must have strength on its own for this to happen.

Cultivate Group Pride vs. Individual Ego

Western media loves to tell stories of lone wolves who have achieved success completely on their own merits. The reality is that this is simply never true. Every person has been influenced by family, friends and colleagues along the way. Even seemingly negative influences have contributed to your learning, to who you are and to what you are able to do today. Start to acknowledge and express gratitude for everyone who has contributed to your achievements.

Take Responsibility

Blame and resentment block harmony, but these cannot exist in the face of radical personal responsibility. You cannot change others or choose how they will treat you, but you can choose how you will react. While it might be difficult initially to control the emotional reactions you have to the people and circumstances in your life, you do have complete control over how you think about these situations and the actions you will take. Focus on doing what you can to strengthen your own character first and you will be sure to see positive changes emerge all around you without your direct efforts.

Choose Kindness

Choosing kindness in your thoughts and actions, even when you are hurt or angry, will always lead to greater harmony. It will help you to be more patient and compassionate, be a better listener and put your interests aside long enough to think about solutions that will meet the needs of the other person as well as your own.

Take Care of Yourself

If you are choosing kindness in thought and action, you will naturally be tuned in to the needs and interests of others — but don't forget to be kind to yourself as well. This is the lesson we can take from airline safety videos: you must put your own air mask on first or you will be in no position to help anyone else. Real life has many competing demands and you can't say yes to everything for the sake of group harmony without depleting yourself. Get clear about the one or two things you must do to keep your pump primed and your energy flowing, and let go of the rest. Your ability to be kind diminishes in direct proportion to your level of exhaustion.

Embrace Conflict

Looking out for your own interests can create conflict, but this does not need to be a bad thing. If we encourage open communication and healthy conflict, individual needs and interests don't need to be subverted. Once out in the open, conflicts can be discussed and creative solutions found that work for everyone. Just as the irritation of the grain of sand is needed to make the pearl, conflict is just an opportunity to create harmony.

Learn to Flow

Harmony, like life, is not a static state. Seasons change and change again. Rocks appear in the river. Water levels rise and fall. Harmony cannot exist in the face of resistance to what is. When you come to expect change, you develop the ability to flow around barriers and roll with the punches in a life that is in constant motion.

The most important thing to remember to build and sustain harmony in your life, your family, your workplace and the world is this: the greater the integrity of the parts, the more vibrant their combined result. This doesn't make the Japanese *wa* that requires people to place individual interests on the back burner in favor of the interests of the group wrong. It simply means that care must be taken to ensure that doing so will strengthen, rather than weaken the individual as well as the group.

It takes time, courage, creativity and commitment to avoid taking shortcuts that will sacrifice either the individual or the group. It is far easier to achieve harmony through forcing ourselves, or others, to be less than they are, to stay silent and to preserve the status quo. But just as one weak part in your body can create a ripple effect of problems in other areas as other parts try to compensate, harmony that is achieved by weakening the parts is destined to fall flat. It may take effort to tune ourselves to this new frequency of the harmony of wholes, but the results will be well worth it.

ELEVEN

The Face of Authenticity

Authenticity
(Shingi)

*Being at peace with yourself to the point that you
no longer feel the need to present anything other
than the real you to the rest of the world.*

People often talk about wanting careers, relationships and
workplaces where they can be themselves, but then lament
that external forces don't allow it. The boss, the boyfriend, the
parent, society, finances — all of these are blamed for why they
can't be their true selves. This is only partly true. The reality is
that human beings both fear and crave authenticity.

In Japanese there are two words that describe this
dichotomy between who we are in public and who we are in
private: *tatemae* and *honne*. *Tatemae* is your public face, your
official stance or how you show your feelings in public. *Honne*
represents your true feelings. The concepts of *tatemae* and
honne are deeply embedded in the Japanese psyche because of
the high value that Japanese culture places on *wa* (harmony).

Many foreigners living in Japan get frustrated by how difficult it is to get behind the the *tatemae* face that a Japanese person shows to the world and connect with the true honne self of their Japanese friends and colleagues.

It is easy to be critical of this aspect of the Japanese culture. As someone from outside it can seem like you are being judged or deliberately kept at a distance. It can feel frustrating when, after being friends with a Japanese person for years, you still do not feel like you really know them.

The reality, however, is that every culture has this difference between public self and private self. It is an integral part of the human experience. It is perfectly natural to put your best self forward in work situations in order to get ahead in your career. It is functional and adaptive to pretend to believe what those around you believe so that you can fit in and benefit from the safety, security and comfort of belonging to a group. While the line between what is public and private varies significantly across cultures, it is human nature to keep certain aspects of ourselves private — even from those we are closest to.

But what happens when your true self remains hidden even from yourself?

Many people go through life kidding themselves about who they really are and what they really want. This is partially due to the fact that it is painful to acknowledge those parts of ourselves that we are not so proud of. The parts that are greedy, selfish, lazy, narcissistic, egotistical, chronically angry, jealous, mean, compulsive, obsessive, illogical and petty. We don't want to acknowledge our dark sides because we fear that doing so makes us weak at best — and downright evil at worst.

The good news is that facing up to your dark side can make you a stronger and better person. No matter how great of a job you do deluding yourself that these negative characteristics don't exist, others around you see them. Those closest to you have likely tried to enlighten you on multiple occasions, but you have managed to ignore their feedback, deny their accusations and, if you are really skillful at self-deception, even turn it around and make it their issue. At some level, however, your subconscious recognizes the truth in what they have said or you wouldn't be going to so much trouble to deny it.

There is a second version of hiding one's true self that is very common. While some spend their lives trying to deny their dark side, others spend their lives wallowing in it. Commonly referred to as low self-esteem, this false sense of being utterly flawed is no more accurate than the picture of oneself as being flawless. Just as those who won't acknowledge their weaknesses are not seeing their true selves, those who refuse to give equal time to their strengths are also hiding from the truth.

Depression, midlife crises, stress, dissatisfaction, boredom, addiction, materialism, isolation — all of these are symptoms of denial of our true selves. People use huge amounts of energy trying to hide from their dark side or deny their magnificence. Facing up to the truth of who you are frees up all of this energy. This energy can then be used to make true progress towards becoming the best person you can be.

Whether the face you put forward is one of false strength or one of false weakness, neither of these is real. True strength comes from learning to look in the mirror and simply acknowledge the reality of what is there — the good, the bad, the ugly and the beautiful.

So the next time you find yourself getting frustrated by the entrenched *tatemae* public face of the people in your life, use it as an opportunity to look at the ways that you are not letting your true self shine through. The more you shift your energy away from them and get back to being more honest with yourself, the more energy, strength and creativity you will free up to live a more authentic, fulfilling and truly prosperous life.

Kyosei as a Personal Practice

Kyosei
Living and working together for the common good.

Living in Japan, I found the desire and ability of Japanese people to function harmoniously as a group to be infinitely fascinating. Far more so than in Western culture, Japanese culture promotes the long-term interests of the group over the short-term interests of the individual. They even have a word for it: *kyosei.*

The word "kyosei" is made up of two characters "kyo" (together) and "sei" (to live). It was first introduced as an academic term in biology to refer to symbiosis. In the 1980s, however, Canon's chairman, Ryuzaburo Kaku, adopted it for use in a business context. As a core of Canon's corporate philosophy, he defined *kyosei* as "living and working together for the common good."

In the early '90s, Kaku's philosophy of *kyosei* was instrumental in developing the Caux Round Table (CRT), and the CRT Principles for Business (a comprehensive set of ethical norms for businesses operating across multiple cultures that has the practice of *kyosei* at their core). These principles have since been published in twelve languages, used in business school curricula worldwide, and become widely recognized as the foundational principles of the corporate social responsibility movement.

Unfortunately, while documents like the CRT Principles do support businesses in practicing *kyosei*, they have one big weakness: they depend on the ability of each individual employee to consistently put them into practice.

Here's the clincher. Like any other rules, the CRT principles are open to interpretation, and interpretation tends to favor self-interest. Knowing what to do is only half of the battle. Doing it is far more difficult. This is why *kyosei*, at its core, is a personal practice, not a business one. If you are passionate about the need for businesses to take the lead in social responsibility and environmental sustainability, it is not enough to sit on the sidelines and cheer or criticize. You can and must contribute by learning what it takes to make daily choices that are in the best long-term interest of both yourself and the whole.

My understanding of what it takes to practice *kyosei* on a personal level is by no means complete, but the following ideas offer a place to start:

1. Seek Knowledge

Thriving on the common good requires that we seek out information, principles and guidelines about how to build a world that generates sustainable prosperity and well-being for all living things. Creating agreement around what information to use, however, is a difficult task as there are many competing schools of thought on how to achieve *kyosei*. The CRT principles, for example, focus on businesses that assume globalization is a virtue. Other organizations would argue that production and consumption must be more localized in order for society to thrive.

It can be frustrating to sort through the conflicting messages out there regarding how to increase well-being for both people and the planet, but don't let this deter you. Being part of the solution requires that you constantly seek to expand your knowledge and skills. Personally, I focus on how exciting it is to see the growing number of people proposing solutions to this challenge, rather than on how frustrating it can be to sort through it all to determine which philosophies to base my actions on.

2. Open Your Mind — and Your Heart

To truly be able to practice *kyosei* you must be willing to entertain the possibility that everything you believe is right could be wrong. Consider the changes that technology has made possible in even the last few decades. When you stop to think for a moment that most of these would have been considered pure science fiction to our grandparents, it becomes easier to suspend judgment and entertain the possibilities of completely new ways of being.

Remember that there was a time when most human beings thought the earth was flat, so consider the possibility that you are arguing vehemently for something that will be proven totally and utterly wrong in the future. Or as Albert Einstein said, "You can't solve problems using the same kind of thinking we used when we created them." Make it a habit to try on new perspectives and challenge yourself to wear them for awhile before deciding that they don't fit. Not only will this give you more clarity on opposing points of view, it will better steel your existing argument should your side need to prevail.

3. Be Mindful of Motivations

We all have legitimate needs like food, clothing, shelter, safety, belonging and love that, when left unmet, challenge our ability to take the higher ground. A person on welfare is less likely to invest time and energy in sourcing ethically produced products than someone who has a good income and time on their hands. That said, examples abound of people who had legitimate reason to take the low road yet chose not to.

For most people in the developed world, however, it is not the basic physical and psychological needs that influence their ability to practice *kyosei*. It is their ego needs for security, comfort, power, status, and control that prevent these choices. The ability to live and work together for the common good depends on each person taking individual responsibility for examining how their self-interest impacts their choices – and having the courage to set aside personal ego needs to pursue a society where everyone thrives. For corporate CEOs, this might mean questioning whether that money they want to spend on buying a company yacht could be put to better use elsewhere. For someone else, it might mean simply taking more time to really listen to others instead of bulldozing their own ideas through.

4. Consider the Consequences to Others

Practicing *kyosei* requires mindfulness. This involves taking the time to consider the consequences your actions will have on others. We can start developing this skill in our children from a very young age. When my four year old doesn't understand why I won't let him pick the flowers in the park, I do what many parents would do and ask him, "What if everyone picked the flowers in the park?" This helps him learn to extrapolate the consequences of his actions beyond his own immediate enjoyment.

The challenge people have in carrying this wisdom forward into adulthood is time. It takes time to slow down long enough to think through to the consequences of our actions. Even more so, it takes time to identify alternate solutions and strategies if the consequences we discover are undesirable. As we grow in the wisdom of seeing ourselves as part of an interconnected whole, rather than as a separate entity, it becomes easier to forgo short-term self-interest and invest the time to find solutions that preserve the integrity of the whole.

5. Energize With Alignment

The final element to consider in growing your ability to practice *kyosei* on a personal level is the need to sustain your energy, commitment and passion for making these types of choices long term. This energy emerges naturally from developing a strong foundation of alignment between who you are and what you do in all areas of your life and work, something I call *Life-Work Integrity*.

Building a strong foundation of *Life-Work Integrity* requires developing an understanding of your personal purpose, values, strengths and vision. Awareness of your strengths increases your ability to spend your time doing things that energize you. Awareness of your values allows you to identify and address integrity gaps before they grow too large. Clarity of vision provides you with the focus that prevents wasted energy from pursuing too many paths. Clarity of purpose provides the reason to persist, even when things get hard.

Applying the above principles and cultivating the ability to practice *kyosei* in life and work ultimately requires a shift in mindset. When people begin to understand that investing time in the right places now saves time and energy over the long term, they develop the ability to "slow down to speed up." As you develop this ability to stop, step back and get curious about the consequences of your choices, you will strengthen your ability to make choices in your life and work that will build a world where everyone thrives.

THIRTEEN

Work Less, Nap More

Sleep
(Suimin)

*The thing most people mistakenly believe they
need to give up in order to be successful.*

Workaholism is a tough habit to break. Why? Unlike drug and alcohol addictions where overdoing it is frowned upon, overwork is considered a badge of honor in many countries. In North America, the greeting "How are you?" is being replaced with "Are you busy?" Just as everyone knows that "fine" is the expected response to the former, the only proper reply to the latter is "yes."

Don't believe me? Try answering "no" and see what happens!

A few years back I did exactly that. After speaking at a conference on the topic of work-life balance, I noticed that not only were others using this greeting pattern more and more frequently, but that I had fallen into it myself. Feeling like a bit of a hypocrite due to the speech I had just given, I quickly concocted a one-week experiment to challenge this unspoken belief that busyness is good.

The experiment had two simple parts: 1) I went back to asking people how they were (and really wanting to know) instead of whether or not they were busy; and 2) If someone asked me if I was busy I replied, "no."

The results were fascinating. When I told people I was not busy I was met with one of two responses: 1) quiet pity that I must somehow be failing in my life and business; or 2) undisguised confusion that I could possibly exist in this world without being busy.

Despite the increased focus on life-work balance in the last decade, it is still common to feel like a bit of a slacker and believe you are destined for failure if you simply work a 40-hour workweek.

In Japan, this belief is alive and well as evidenced by their tolerance of *inemuri*, the practice of sleeping on the job. Rather than being seen as a sign of laziness, it is seen as a sign of commitment! If you need to sleep at work, the thinking goes, it must mean that you are super-dedicated and putting in such long hours that you don't have time to sleep at home.

North America is no different. For many years, Sheryl Sandberg, now the COO of Facebook, hid the fact that she left the office every day by 5:30. She was worried that people would question her competence as a leader for doing so.

The idea that long hours demonstrate greater commitment and lead to greater success is founded on the misguided belief that the more hours a person works, the more they get done. This is simply not true. Decades of research have proven that working more than 40 hours per week on an ongoing basis decreases productivity. The Ford Motor Company didn't arbitrarily institute a 40-hour workweek in the 1900s — it was based on dozens of tests showing that working longer decreased productivity and increased errors.

The bottom line: The most successful and dedicated employees have an obligation to restrict themselves to an 8-hour work day. It ensures productivity and sustains their ability to be innovative and effective both in the short term and in the long run.

Does this mean napping at work is on the way out? Fortunately not!

Research by NASA has concluded that the more complex your work, the more beneficial napping during the day is to improving focus and productivity. Even if you aren't into napping, you might want to re-visit the idea that dedicated employees must skip lunch and breaks to optimize their productivity. Research on ultradian rhythms (biological cycles that repeat daily) and productivity, suggests that people are more creative and perform best when they work in three-hour blocks with a half hour rest in between. Psychologist Mihaly Csikszentmihalyi, author of Flow, suggests that blocks of 90 minutes are the ideal period between breaks for optimizing attention, focus, flow and innovation.

We all clearly need to re-examine our beliefs about what commitment, dedication and success look like. Lucky for us, the science supports what social pressure does not: what is good for people is actually good for business too.

FOURTEEN

A New Perspective on Planning

Plan
(Keikaku)

*Something you feel strangely good about having despite
the fact that life often keeps you from following it.*

I have long believed that taking the time to clarify your vision,
set goals and map out strategies to get from where you are to
where you want to be is an essential ingredient for success, but
2014 made me question that philosophy.

Typically we take part in a major planning session at
the end of each year, but in the last few weeks of 2013, my
husband (who is also my business partner) came down with
an eye infection so serious we thought he might go blind. He
recovered, but we did not have time to do our usual annual
planning before the holidays. We scheduled to do it first thing
in January instead, but life had other plans.

On January 4th, we found out my older brother, still
only in his forties, had cancer. Nine days later, my husband's
grandmother passed away unexpectedly. My brother died two

weeks after that. My mother had just moved to Vancouver and was staying with us while she found a place, but my brother's death turned what was supposed to be a two-month stay into nine months. To top it all off, I ended up spending more than three months dealing with a breast cancer scare and recovering from a seriously botched biopsy.

Despite all of this, we somehow managed to have an amazing year in business, hiring two new employees, completing a record number of projects, and doubling our revenues. As this had occurred without our usual strategic planning, I became curious about whether or not our traditional goal-setting processes were actually instrumental to our success.

Looking back I realized that, despite our lack of formal planning, we did already have plans, goals and project management systems in place that carried through from the year before. These, together with our pre-existing vision for our lives and business continued to provide us with the focus and direction we needed to stay on track in the face of our personal challenges. Because of this, I realized that I couldn't attribute our achievements to a complete lack of planning. Still, I knew something was different.

I realized that there were several big changes I had made because of my brother's death that had allowed us to achieve much more that year than we had in any previous year.

I Slowed Down, Tuned In,
and Stayed in the Moment

I took far more time than usual to think about my true purpose and priorities in life and work. I wrote in my journal, went for more walks in nature and spent more time focused on what I was feeling in the moment. I spent less time thinking about what I had to do and worrying about the future. At first it was just because I didn't have energy to do anything other than deal with my grief. Gradually, however, this turned into a greater sense of connection with my intuition, my strengths, and my passions. The more I acted on what I was feeling drawn to do in the moment, the more it seemed that my actions generated results beyond my expectations.

I Let Go of Anything That Was Not Essential

To fulfill my roles as a wife, mother, daughter and business partner while accounting for the toll that grief took, some things had to give. I finally gave myself permission to say no and go back on commitments without guilt, reducing my networking events and social engagements by 80%. The more I stepped outside of the usual busyness, the more I started to connect with what was most important. When I stepped into the business, I did only those things that were truly important and urgent. This created better results despite less activity.

I Stopped Trying to Control Everything

I simply did not have the energy to be involved in every decision. To my surprise, decisions got made, stuff got done and everyone stressed less. Some mistakes were made, but the time we saved more than made up for the time spent fixing and learning from challenges.

I Realized That Bigger Is Not Better

In years past we put a lot of pressure on ourselves to make massive progress. Out of necessity in 2014 we focused on small, achievable actions. We stressed less, easily exceeded our targets and enjoyed greater energy and confidence from setting and achieving smaller goals. Reflecting on this changed our planning process for the following year. We did set business goals, but we let go of the notion that we were completely in control. We kept our goals small and our milestones reasonable. The atmosphere in the office was calmer, happier, more focused and, as a result, more productive.

As surprising as this might seem, research actually supports it. Goals become counterproductive if they are too big or deadlines too aggressive because it increases stress to the point that it impedes performance.

On a personal level, that year forced me to consider that part of the reason people don't achieve their goals is because they have too many of them. Instead of setting goals, I now set simple intentions about how I want to be. Then I put action behind these intentions with very small daily habits. If, for example, I get up by 5am, I know I have the energy to do everything I want. By committing to the habit of being asleep by 10pm on weekdays, I don't need a concrete plan for what I will do at 5am, I just know that good things happen in my head and my life when I am up early. The first good domino topples the next.

If you're tired of the massive push to do great things, and beginning to worry that you will (again) fail to achieve your goals this year, slow down to consider what is really important, how you want to be different, and the small goals and habits that will have the biggest positive impact in your life. When you begin to focus on small achievable input activities, rather than huge, daunting, outcomes, you will surprise yourself — and everyone else — with what you can achieve.

FIFTEEN

Buddhism, Braces and Balance

Balance
(Heikō)

Something to stop longing for, as it is actually what's keeping you from having the life you want.

In today's fast-paced world, even the wealthiest people say they would love more of one thing: balance. The challenge? Balance, by definition, is about maintaining a state of equilibrium that is stable and unchanging. People who want more balance in their lives and work don't want things to stay the same. They want them to change. More balance to most means having more time and/or money to spend on health, family, hobbies, relaxation, or moving a dream forward. Unfortunately, their lives are already "balanced" in a state of equilibrium that doesn't allow for these pursuits.

The problem, then, with the quest for balance is that you already have it. What you really want is more energy, joy, vitality, success and fulfillment. You don't want balance, you want to thrive! In order to thrive, you need to stop striving for more balance and learn to actively shift the existing balance in your life towards your new desired set point.

Strangely, I happened across the perfect explanation of how to shift out of balance and into thriving during a visit to my orthodontist. Due to a freak accident where I got hit in the face while meditating (yes, meditating!) I had to get braces to reposition my teeth in preparation for a dental implant. After taking pictures and molds of my teeth, the orthodontist explained the process I would be going through over the next year like this:

"Except for the recent injury" he said, "your teeth are currently in perfect equilibrium. Even though your bite is not optimal and your teeth are not perfectly straight they have achieved their own balance and stability. Once we begin moving things around, this balance will be upset and the changes will need to be monitored closely to ensure that movement is occurring in the desired direction. We won't know exactly how the other teeth will shift in response to shifting the ones we need to at the front. Sometimes it will seem that we are undoing something that we just did, but don't worry. As long as we have a clear picture of where we started and a clear vision of the end result we want to create, we will keep fine-tuning until eventually we reach the goal. For this reason, the time estimate I am giving you for the complete process may not be 100% accurate, but based on my experience and barring any unforeseen difficulties, it will not be too far off. You will experience some pain and discomfort during the process as your teeth move but the worst of this will be at the early stages when the movement is greatest. Once you are finished you will need to wear a retainer of some kind for several years and possibly for life to prevent your teeth from moving back to their original position."

Listening to his words I was hit with a flash of insight. Braces provide the perfect illustration of how to build your capacity to thrive in all areas of your life and work! Unbeknownst to my orthodontist, his comments illustrated eight core principles of shifting balance and learning to thrive:

1. Every Element of Your Life and Work Is Already in Balance, Even Though You May Not Like What That Balance Is

A balanced state is not desirable in and of itself. The most obvious example of this is body weight. Many people have maintained a stable weight for many years that is 10, 20 or even 30 pounds over their ideal weight. While they may not like the way they look or feel at this weight, it is perfectly balanced with the type and amount of food they eat, the amount of exercise they get and their metabolism.

Another example of a stable or balanced state people find themselves in is an unhealthy relationship. We all know of people who have been in a long-term relationship with an established status quo that is dysfunctional. While neither party may be all that happy, they have a stable pattern in the relationship. Despite not being particularly healthy, you cannot deny that their relationship has achieved a balanced state.

2. Changing Anything Causes Everything to Shift (Whether You Want It to or Not)

David Klein's now-classic study of the reindeer on St. Matthew Island illustrates the principles of balance in operation. In 1944 a population of just 29 animals was moved to an island where the species did not previously exist. The absence of predators such as wolves and human hunters caused the population to swell to 6000 in 19 years. Then, within a space of 3 years, the population crashed to 41 females and one male, all in miserable condition. Klein originally estimated that the carrying capacity of the island was about 5 deer per square kilometer. At the population peak there were 18 per square kilometer, but after the crash there were only 0.126 per kilometer. Klein projected that the original carrying capacity would take decades to return even without any deer because a key source of food production (lichens) had been eliminated.

By now our awareness of environmental issues has made it common knowledge that introducing even the smallest change or a seemingly harmless element (such as reindeer) into a complex system can upset the balance. The same applies to all areas of your own life and work. This explains why your attempts at balancing your life to make it better can sometimes prove so frustrating. Unless you have a top-level understanding of every possible link and interconnection within a complex system, it is impossible to know what the repercussions of any single choice will be. The old adage that things often "get worse before they get better" also comes into play. The reactions and consequences created by the system trying to either return to its previous state of equilibrium or a new state of equilibrium are not always positive or comfortable in the present.

One of the key sources of stress in people's lives and work is their resistance to this constantly shifting balance. External forces are constantly acting upon individuals and organizations causing change, so, no matter how much balance you have created in your own life, the external balance will constantly be shifting, causing your balance to be upset. Learning to handle and enjoy the process of constantly shifting the balance is critical for learning to thrive.

3. To Succeed, You Need to Have a Clear Picture of Where You Are and Where You Want to Go

Most people have a very vague picture of what success looks like, who they are and where they really want to go. Young people starting out in their first career have hopes that it will be a vehicle to provide health, wealth, happiness and the fulfillment of their dreams. Unfortunately, most people lose sight of these hopes early on. Instead they get sucked into the prevailing mindset of pushing, struggling and striving to do more, have more and earn more at an ever increasing pace. They get caught up in keeping up, but lose sight of who they are and what truly makes them happy. Without the latter, achieving the former becomes impossible.

It is all too common to set goals based on what you are told you should want and what you need to do to get there by parents, friends and society. Only in the rarest of cases does this match with the your own intrinsic vision of who you want to be. If you are heading towards a goal that has been dictated by someone else, you will lack the energy and motivation needed to carry you through the hard times on the road to success. Even if you do manage to force yourself to completion, you will find that the goal does not provide the rewards you had hoped it would. Shifting your balance to where you want it to be requires taking the time to craft a clear vision of where you want to go that is based on your authentic needs, personality and passions.

4. You Need to Exert Constant Pressure, Using the Appropriate Skills, Knowledge and Tools, to Shift From Point A to Point B

Our society today is ridden with stress because we have become almost too good at exerting constant pressure on ourselves to do more, be more and have more. Unfortunately most people lack the proper skills, knowledge and tools to exert this pressure correctly and consistently enough to achieve results. They also don't understand how to do so without causing harm to themselves (or others) along the way.

My orthodontist had a variety of tools to achieve the result he was aiming for. He knew exactly which tool to use at which stage of the process in order to shift my teeth from where they were to where he wanted them to be. Your attempts to shift the balance in your life are doomed to fail if you are using tools for one thing that were meant for another. You can use the back of a screwdriver instead of a hammer to pound a nail once, but try to use it to build a whole house and you're going to have problems.

In the same vein, pushing yourself to work harder is not always the answer. Persistence, determination, and long hours are good tools to have in your toolbox, but they aren't always effective. Frequently, they are a crutch of martyrdom. Sometimes you need to call upon other tools such as patience, inspiration, creativity and even fun to get where you want to go. Shifting the balance requires constantly expanding your tool set and learning to use the right tools to adjust your strategies along the way. This allows you to achieve more with less effort (and more fun!).

5. Making the Shift Will Be Uncomfortable, Especially at First

Change becomes less uncomfortable over time as you get used to it. When I had braces, the first few days after each adjustment would be painful as my teeth shifted. As the process wore on, each adjustment was less painful and the discomfort lasted for shorter periods of time.

The discomfort associated with shifting the balance in your life will also decrease over time. Once movement is underway, you are not as attached to (or stuck in) your old ways of doing and being. Newton's first law of motion states that "an object at rest tends to stay at rest and an object in motion tends to stay in motion." Once you are in motion, it is more comfortable and easier to stay in motion. Plus, as you see progress towards your goal, you establish a positive feedback loop that reinforces and builds yet more progress.

One of my Buddhism teachers in Japan was fond of a saying: "pain is inevitable, suffering is optional." It wasn't until I went on my first ten-day silent meditation retreat that I began to understand what he was talking about. As I deepened my meditation practice, I discovered a strange kind of pleasure in being able to be with my pain, notice it, and not attach to it in a way that created suffering.

You can see a similar principle in elite athletes. Athletes who are in training know that a certain amount of pain is a sign of progress. They expect and even enjoy it because they know that those sore muscles today will become even stronger by tomorrow. As you develop a thrive mindset, you become like an elite athlete — you welcome the good type of pain that comes from developing yourself in ways that help you reach your goals of superior performance.

This pain factor is one of the key reasons that it is important to seek support in shifting the balance. My orthodontist told me that sometimes a patient would come back after a few weeks and ask to have their braces removed because it was just too painful. He was always able to talk them out of it, and true to his promise, the pain eventually lessened and the patient was glad they had persevered. Having a support network that will keep you from removing your own braces is essential to make it through those times when you want to throw in the towel.

6. You Can't Predict How Long It Will Take to Make the Shift or How It Will Look in Between

This is another good reason to have a support network in place, ideally made up of someone who has the expertise and experience to help you through it. I trusted my orthodontist to make the changes necessary along the way so that I could get from where I was to where I wanted to be. Despite his knowledge, however, he could not predict exactly how long it would take. His estimate turned out to be quite accurate because he has had experience with cases similar to mine, but he warned me that every patient was unique in terms of where they started and where they were going, so guarantees were not possible. The best support person for you is the person who has the skills, knowledge and experience related to the change you are trying to make.

7. You Need to Have Confidence in the Person in Charge of Orchestrating the Shift

With my braces, I was 100% confident that the orthodontist knew what he was doing. He had worked with thousands of patients and had a proven track record of getting great results. This was extremely important since, in other areas of my life, I am not the most patient person.

This impatience is most pronounced and painful in areas where I am trying something new. Despite spending time researching and developing new skills, until I have achieved success in a new area at least once, I find it difficult to trust that I will achieve success at all. This self-doubt increases my impatience because I need external validation that I am doing things right. In the case of my braces, it was easy to be patient because I trusted that my orthodontist knew what we was doing and would get me where I wanted to go.

In your life, you may have had more experience with not getting the results you desire because you don't understand the above principles. Once you understand that balance is working against you, that you need to exert effort to overcome this balance, that it is going to be chaotic along the way and that you can't predict how long it will take to reach your goal, it becomes easier to persist. This understanding allows you to reframe the pain and the mess as signs of progress rather than signs of failure.

8. You Will Need Systems, Tools and Habits to Maintain the New State of Equilibrium

Just as I still need to wear my retainer at night to keep my teeth from shifting, it is not enough to shift the balance. You must put the proper habits, tools and systems in place to ensure you are able to sustain your new state of balance over time. With time and practice, your new equilibrium will become the norm. You will form new thought habits and, just like driving a car, you will eventually be able to drive while also being able to enjoy the scenery around you.

With this new perspective on balance as a process to master, rather than a goal to achieve, you will be in a much better position to achieve your goals in life with less stress, greater ease, and more fun than ever before.

SIXTEEN

The Year of Alignment

Death
(Shi)

A permanent condition you long for when work sucks the life out of you.

Living in modern society is tough.

It is stressful. A 2015 global survey of 1000 corporations across 15 countries commissioned by The Regus Group found that 6 in 10 workers have experienced increased stress in the last two years.

It is soul killing. According to the Gallup organization's 2015 Global Workplace Report conducted in 142 countries, only 13% of employees are truly engaged in their jobs. That leaves 63% who are just "showing up," and a whopping 24% who are negative, miserable and, worst of all, actively spreading their misery around!

It is potentially deadly. In Japan, *karōshi* (death from overwork) and *karojisatsu* (suicide from overwork and stressful working conditions) are still prevalent. Official statistics from the Japanese government cite *karōshi* as a cause of death for nearly 300 people each year. Of the 30,000 plus suicides each year, many are attributed to overwork and other employment conditions.

You might argue that the underlying causes of these statistics are external factors such as the economy, corporate policies or inept managers that are beyond the control of the average person, but you would only be partly right. There is actually something you can do to take control of your life and thrive even in the most difficult times: align with your authentic core.

Your authentic core comprises four key areas: values, strengths, purpose and vision. Defining and aligning with each one of them provides different benefits that help to combat stress, increase health and build foundations for lasting happiness and fulfillment.

Align With Your Strengths

Living with stress drains your energy. When your energy reserves are low, it is difficult to take any positive action to address the sources of stress in your life. This is where your strengths come in.

Spending time doing things that are aligned with your strengths is inherently energizing. Think about it: How do you feel after spending a long day doing something that you love? You might be physically tired, but, at some level, you will also feel energized. I like to call this "good tired."

Contrast this with spending a whole day (or maybe even an hour) doing something that you don't like and aren't good at. Personally, I get exhausted just thinking about doing my own bookkeeping!

Aligning with your strengths provides the energy you need to combat the inevitable stresses of things that are beyond your control. Spend some time getting clear on the things that you love to do so much that a whole day spent doing them leaves you feeling energized rather than tired. Then make a plan to do more of those activities. Next, make a list of all of the activities that you don't like, that you aren't (and don't want to be) good at, and that you find draining. Figure out ways you can eliminate, delegate or minimize these activities as much as possible.

This will give you energy for discovering and aligning with the next element of your authentic core: your values.

Align With Your Values

Values misalignment is one of the biggest sources of stress in a person's life. Your values are like promises you have made to yourself. When your actions (or the actions of those around you) are not aligned with these values, you feel the same about yourself as you would about anyone else who constantly broke promises to you. While you can't change other people's values, you can limit the energy you lose from values misalignment by becoming more aware of your own values.

When you take the time to clearly define your values in writing, it becomes evident which values are being compromised by the stressful situations in your life or work. Once you understand where the stress is coming from, it becomes easier to create strategies to address the circumstances that are responsible.

Note that it is not enough to simply pick words off a list of values from a book. This is better than nothing, but the real value in identifying your values comes from taking the time to clearly define what your life, work and relationships look like when they are in alignment with these values. This does take some time to do, but the dividends are huge. Clients I've helped report that just four sessions on clarifying their values had a transformational impact on their ability to resolve stress in their lives.

Align With Your Purpose

More research is constantly emerging to prove that a strong sense of purpose drives happiness, health and success. A strong sense of purpose provides the enthusiasm and hope to persist even when external challenges appear. Believing that what you are doing has meaning beyond just making money or satisfying your own needs is also deeply energizing at a spiritual level. Long hours worked in service of the greater good are energizing. Long hours worked to make money, meet obligations, or just to pay the bills drain your body and your soul to the core.

Align With Your Vision

The final element of your authentic core is a clear vision. Having a clear vision for your future provides direction, energy and focus despite the abundant distractions that come your way on a daily basis. If you do not have a clear vision (or do not consciously refer to your vision daily), you are being more driven by other people's visions than your own. While you still might need to comply with your company's vision to keep your job, having a clear vision for what you want to achieve in your work makes it far more likely that you will meet both their goals and your own.

Whether you are having a personal energy crisis, or simply looking to feel more alive, a focus on discovering your authentic core and increasing your alignment with it will take you there. Commit to making this your year of alignment, and get ready to enjoy greater energy, vitality and passion in all areas of your life and work.

SEVENTEEN

Don't Sweat the Small Stuff

Focus
(Shūchū)

The thing you lose when you try to do it all.

In our industry, August and September are usually slow from a work perspective. Many clients postpone sessions due to holidays or because they are busy ramping their families up for fall. For this reason, we also take advantage of this slow time to go on vacation and enjoy the summer weather.

One year, we unexpectedly had a large influx of new clients itching to get started and ramp up in August. While excited to start working with new people, we also had two vacations and lots of fun summer activities planned, so it did tax our resources. As August rolled on, I found my stress level rising despite all of the time off we were taking.

Since the work I do with clients to better manage their time and energy centers on understanding priorities, I soon realized our unexpectedly high client load meant I was going to need to make some choices. Not wanting to give up the fun summer activities with my family, I began postponing non-critical tasks to reduce my commitments. What I hadn't done, I realized, was to reduce my expectations of myself.

Despite outwardly re-prioritizing and de-committing, inwardly I felt guilty for doing so. I felt bad for postponing meetings. I worried about being seen as unprofessional for making clients wait while I went on vacation. I was stressed about neglecting my regular house-cleaning routine even though I had consciously decided beach picnics were more of a priority than clean floors. In short, I was most definitely sweating the small stuff!

One day at the beach, a friend made the offhand comment that I seemed pretty stressed for someone who was taking so much time off. As I sat there on the gorgeous beach watching our kids frolic in the water, it dawned on me that I was nowhere near the present moment. I was so busy in my head thinking about the things I was going to need to do later, that I wasn't reaping the benefits of the choices I had made to re-prioritize tasks so I could enjoy the summer as much as my increased client load would allow.

I was reminded of a Zen parable about two monks walking through the woods. As they are walking, the monks come upon a stream. Beside it they see a beautiful woman in distress because she can't cross the stream without getting her kimono wet. Without a thought, the older monk picks her up and carries her across the stream. Deeply grateful, the woman continues on her way and the monks continue along theirs.

Several hours later, the younger monk, obviously stressed, berates the older monk saying, "Brother, I can't believe that you picked up that woman and carried her across the stream.

This goes against our vows of celibacy to not have any contact with the opposite sex."

"Brother," the older monk replies, "I only held her for a few moments as I lifted her across the stream. You have been carrying her the whole afternoon."

Like the younger monk, I was having a hard time letting go of all of my "shoulds." Even though I had let go of the activities themselves, I hadn't released the expectations I had of myself that went with those activities. Like the younger monk, I was still carrying the activities with me even though I was not doing them.

Whether you are having a busy season or a busy life, the first step to preserving your vitality and maintaining your sanity is to remember that you cannot do it all. To determine what to keep and what to toss, slow down long enough to ask yourself the following questions:

- What is my ideal vision for this season (or my life, work, or family)?
- What values and principles do I most want to live by?
- Which activities am I involved in that are most aligned with the above? Which are least aligned? Which are not aligned at all?

With these questions, most of my clients find it becomes immediately obvious which of the things they are trying to pack in to their lives and work really matter and which don't. It is hard to back out of commitments, but, ultimately, this allows you to focus your energy where it will really make a difference for you and those around you.

The second, more difficult step is to let go of the expectations and self-judgment that go with all of the things you did not choose. Remember: without letting go of the things you didn't choose, you cannot truly be free to savor the ones you did.

How do you know whether you have let go or not? If you are feeling guilty or stressed in any way about your choices, you haven't fully made peace with them.

Not sure how to make the shift? Awareness is the first step. Sometimes just being aware that you are holding on to expectations is enough to release these judgments of yourself. If that doesn't work, spend some time reviewing how the things you chose support your vision and values, and how the things you released were unimportant, non-essential, or even completely off track.

Finally, take time to consider the possibility that the space you vacated is now open to be filled by someone who will truly benefit from that activity.

Fear is ultimately the thing that keeps us stuck doing things that aren't a good fit. Whether you are afraid of missing out or afraid of being judged by yourself or others, actions that are motivated by fear are guaranteed to create a life of stress. The good news is that the more you have the courage to step through fear and make choices that align with your authentic self, the more you will experience that all of those things you fear will never come to pass.

EIGHTEEN

Tsubos, Spirit and Success

Spirit
(Seishin)
*The force within you that gives the body
its life, energy and power.*

Writing resumés (and, more recently, building LinkedIn profiles) is symbolic of mass society, stuck in the past and focused on the way things have always been done. Resumés are more interested in what people have done than in who they are today. We have been taught that building careers and accumulating material status is necessary for success, happiness and fulfillment.

But all that is changing. People who have reached these career peaks are discovering that, despite having the toys and the title, they are left strangely unfulfilled. Yet most people continue to do more of the same. Why? They aren't aware that there is another option.

People choose building career, status and material possessions by default because that is what they are told success means. They are taught that hard work, competition and pushing yourself are the route to success. They are told that success involves only external measures of material success, not internal measures of spiritual fulfillment. These approaches work, but they have a cost. They bring stress, depression, overwork and imbalance.

Crafting your spirit requires a radically different way of thinking. It requires a commitment to personal integrity and accountability. It demands that you face fears, step beyond ego defenses and give up the need to be right. It challenges you to constantly cultivate an awareness of your highest and basest motivations. It calls on you to find the courage to follow your own unique path, despite judgment, criticism and disapproval from others. It requires patience, constant openness to feedback, the willingness to adjust and a commitment to constantly fine-tune awareness.

Crafting your spirit is tricky. It reminds me of studying *shiatsu* massage when I lived in Kyoto. In *shiatsu*, a *tsubo* is a spot on one of the body's meridians that is raised, indented or hardened. It indicates an imbalance or a blockage. These are the points where pressure needs to be applied to release blocked energy and restore health.

One of the interesting things about *tsubos* is that they move. When I placed my finger or elbow on a *tsubo* at a particular angle, it would only stay there so long before it would subtly move or quickly pop out from under my healing pressure. I had to release my pressure and come back at it again from another angle. Sometimes a particular *tsubo* would shift five or six times. I had to go back again and again before it was fully released.

Achieving success with soul requires the application of similar principles in your life. You must look for those places where you are hardened, your energy is blocked or you are not in the flow. You must then apply pressure over time to them from many angles to heal them. Healing these blocks can be painful and requires the skill to apply the right type of pressure, the willingness to release old habits and the creativity and commitment to persevere in applying healing pressure from different angles over time. If you lack the skill, willingness, courage or persistence you will not be able to release these old patterns and achieve success and fulfillment on your own terms.

To determine some of the areas where you might be focused more on writing your resumé than on crafting your spirit, consider the following questions:

- Am I pursuing this opportunity for the money, power or status it affords despite the feeling that my heart is not in it?
- Am I taking this career path to please anyone other than myself?
- Do I believe that what I really want to do will not pay enough, not be respected by others or in some other way have a negative consequence?
- If I knew that fulfillment in my work was about changing something in me, not changing my job, what would I need to change?

The answers that you receive to these questions are the *tsubos* that you must begin to apply healing pressure to. You will work on them from one direction and they will move. You will forget about them for awhile, thinking that they have disappeared. You will change your mind about whether you want to heal them at all. You will get tired. You will lose hope. You will find hope and start again. Slowly, bit by bit, resumés and artful LinkedIn profiles will become a thing of the past. You will find a new definition of success. One that is based in the peace and contentment that can only come from a deep confidence in your ability to craft your spirit, not to market it.

NINETEEN

The Price of Letting Go

Letting Go
(Tebanasu)

*The skill and wisdom of releasing some of what you
have to make room for more of what you want.*

Successful people often attribute their success to the tenacity
with which they hold onto their vision, their principles and
their ideas about the right and wrong way to do things. Yet it is
precisely this attachment to beliefs, ideas, and even visions that
also stops them from reaching the next level of achievement in
their life and work.

Consider the accounting student who succeeds in
completing school and getting a job despite realizing half-way
through her studies that she doesn't enjoy accounting. She
followed through on her goal but set herself up for a career
that will never bring her joy. Likewise, a business owner whose
sense of loyalty prevents him from firing an underperforming
employee is contributing to his own limitations.

While the follow-through, loyalty and perseverance demonstrated above are good qualities, they can have negative consequences. Understanding when to hold on and when to let go is a critical skill for balancing success and fulfillment.

To identify where you might need to let go, consider the following three areas:

People

The factor that is most likely to stall individual or business growth is people who are not a good fit. Letting go of people is hard. Firing an employee and divorcing a spouse carry obvious costs and consequences that make people reluctant to go down these paths, but the cost of keeping these relationships around is even greater. While there is little research on the hard costs of keeping an ill-fitting friend or spouse in your life, leading research on employee retention provides some insight. Getting rid of a low-performing employee increases morale and productivity dramatically — even without hiring a suitable replacement.

Take stock of your own relationships and consider how much happier and more productive you could be if you let go of the relationships that take far more of your time and energy than they give back.

Goals

While sticking to your goals is celebrated as a noble character trait, sticking to them when you realize they are no longer a fit is just plain silly. The challenge lies in discerning when it is time to re-commit and when it is time to switch tracks. Many of my "chronic" career changing clients come to me feeling judged by others for not committing to one thing and sticking with it. Once they find the right thing to commit to, however, following through on the hard work necessary to make it happen becomes much easier.

Take a moment to review the goals you are working towards. Ask yourself which you feel genuinely drawn to and which just feel like "shoulds." The goals that are most likely to generate both success and fulfillment are the ones that inspire you, not the ones that feel like "shoulds."

Strategies

This is the final area that gets in the way of people and organizations achieving their full potential. From a business perspective, it might be an unwillingness to let go of a core product, a method of providing service, a way of booking appointments, a manufacturing or quality control process or any other strategy that represents the status quo you have grown comfortable with. On a personal level, it could be anything from believing that you need to own a car to using anger to get your way in your relationships. It could even be a belief that work is meant to be hard and fun is meant only for the weekends.

Your beliefs dictate and limit the strategies you will or won't use, so this is where you need to start to look if you want to get better results. Challenge yourself to look at every aspect of your life and work and ask, "What if everything I thought was right was wrong? What if my old strategies no longer worked? How else could I achieve my objectives? What might a more elegant strategy consist of?" This type of thinking will help you to break through limitations and find new ways of doing that will expose limited thinking, foster creative solutions and create breakthroughs to new levels of happiness and prosperity.

One final thought: the price of letting go is never as steep as you fear. It is the price of holding on to something that is no longer working that will ultimately break both the bank and your heart.

TWENTY

Becoming You

Truth

(Shinjitsu)

*The things your heart usually tells you that
your head doesn't want to hear.*

Many of my Western friends found life in Japan frustrating because the culture was so different from their own that they just couldn't fit in. I found living and working in a foreign culture to be freeing. Rather than feeling like I had to become more Japanese, I embraced Japanese culture and customs as a way of experiencing what it was like to be less Western and find where the real me fit. I knew that no matter how great my spoken Japanese was, or how long I had been there, I would never really be able to fit in or succeed on Japanese terms as a foreigner. So I simply made my own terms.

Eventually, after five fulfilling years, I reached the point where I knew it was time to leave Japan. But just as I was preparing to leave, something unexpected happened. I was offered a job.

Having been an entrepreneur since my early twenties, jobs don't normally tempt me, but this one was different. It was a leadership role, the money was great, it was work I would enjoy, the company fit my values and, most importantly for me at that time, I would have opportunity to travel to Europe, Asia and even Australia and New Zealand. The latter was especially appealing as I knew that my inner passion scales had recently tipped from feeling more alive inside Japan to feeling more alive outside of Japan. While I felt in my heart that Canada was calling me to return and continue building my business there, everything about the opportunity seemed too good to turn down, so I accepted the job.

Having made an uneasy truce with myself, I started the job and silently battled my growing dissatisfaction with Tokyo and my desire to return to Canada. Several months into my new job, a co-worker unknowingly provided the proverbial "last straw" that forced me to realize it really was time for me to go.

Discussing our daily commute, I was bemoaning the discomfort of a 45-minute full-contact ride crammed in with strangers from neck to ankle on all sides. My colleague, Mayumi, told me that I should be happy as her commute was over two hours each way. "Andrea-san," she laughed, "you just need to become more Japanese."

Her off-hand comment haunted me all the way home and to work on my crowded commute for several days. I knew she was right. To stay in Tokyo, to stay in this job, I had to become more Japanese. It would help me to be successful, but, more importantly, I knew it was critical for me to be happy. I had seen this process in other foreign friends who had stayed in Japan for many years. Somewhere around the five or six year mark they all made that internal shift to become more Japanese. Those that didn't make the shift but stayed anyways seemed miserable and stuck. I knew I could make the shift too, but I had to ask: did I want to?

In order to be true to my principles of not compromising my passions, I had to admit that this was a shift I did not want to make. While I had loved my time in Japan and in many ways already had become more Japanese, I knew that I had taken all that I was meant to take from my Japan experiences. I had to let this opportunity go. The job and my life in Japan was a good thing, *but it was not my good thing.*

This was an agonizing choice. I was giving up a guaranteed opportunity for money, travel, status, learning and building my career for the far more difficult and uncertain option of returning to Canada to rebuild my business in a whole new city where I knew no one.

This was just one of the thousands of similar choices I have made along my journey to discover how to be successful without compromising the essence of who I am. Many of these choices have involved giving up the "sure thing" option to take the longer route of finding my own way. Some people might say that I am stubborn and am making things more difficult than they have to be (and many people have). They may be right. My business might have grown faster if I had copied the models that others have used for success. Revenues might grow faster if I were to use some of the sales tactics that, while proven effective, feel unethical to me. It may have taken me longer to reach certain milestones than others have, but in staying true to myself along the way, I have built a stronger foundation to sustain my success than if I had done it their way.

The dreaded midlife crisis that many of my clients come to me to help them through is another manifestation of this same dilemma. It is precipitated by a belief that if they just "become more Japanese" they will be successful and happy. They get into careers that their families approve of. They do what they are told. They achieve their goals. They get the promotion and the raise and the house and all the other things they are told they should want, only to discover that they aren't happy. How could they be if they have been ignoring the internal signs pointing them towards who they really are and what they really want to do along the way?

Whether you are an entrepreneur, a CEO, a janitor or a stay-at-home-parent, you can begin building a stronger foundation now by asking yourself these questions:

- Where am I making choices just so I can fit in?
- Where am I looking to others for a model of success instead of discovering my own?
- Where am I fighting an uphill battle trying to be something that I don't really want to be, and will be miserable trying to become?
- Where might I be fooling myself into thinking that I am taking the short route by doing it someone else's way first so that I can create the "success" I need to do it my way later?

When faced with those choices that you must make each day, ask yourself if you are trying to "become more Japanese," or to become more you? The surest route to success on your own terms — the kind of success that brings abundance not only financially, but physically, socially, and spiritually — is at once the easiest and the hardest thing to do. But it is worth it, every step of the way.

TWENTY ONE

To Eat or not to Eat?
That is the Question

Environment
(Kankyō)

*The surroundings within which you contain
your life that have the potential to either support
or distract you in living your purpose.*

In my efforts to eliminate the last ten pounds I gained while pregnant with our son, I spent the last few years trying every diet imaginable. Despite modest success, I seemed unable to stick to one for any length of time, and was constantly on the hunt for something that would work better or be easier. As each diet had its own version of what to eat, avoid, count and curb, this diet experimentation caused me considerable confusion over what I should or shouldn't eat.

As I also began to notice that I was having issues with low energy and poor digestion, I sought the services of a holistic nutritionist. I was excited about her recommendations, but as they went counter to the rules of "healthy" eating proposed by the diets I had been on before, I once again found myself feeling confused about what really was the best way for me to eat.

In discussing this with my husband, I commented that when I lived in Japan I was the lowest weight and highest energy I had ever been, yet it had seemed effortless to maintain. He asked me a very profound question: What made it so easy for you to eat in a way that felt good in Japan?

I realized that there were two factors. Both my external and internal environments had supported me in adopting a style of eating that felt good for me physically and spiritually.

In the external environment, certain foods such as the Western-style breads and cheeses that I liked were either unavailable or cost prohibitive, so I eliminated them. I found Japanese-style coffee too strong for my taste and Starbucks lattes were nonexistent, so I embraced green tea.

My environment also made it easier to eat in a way that was in alignment with my values, thus increasing my energy in ways that went beyond simple physical health. My closest friends were very health- and environment-conscious. When we went out to eat, it was at places that served healthy organic food. In addition, because they tended to be cheaper, I naturally gravitated towards fruit and veggies that were local and in season. Not only was this a healthier way to eat physically, it felt energizing to be doing something good for the planet as well.

Finally, while in Japan, I began studying Buddhism and practicing meditation on a regular basis. As mindfulness became part of my everyday life, this external influence shifted my internal environment to the point that I was acutely aware of how the foods I consumed impacted my body. I stopped drinking alcohol when I noticed that even a few sips instantly started to make me feel tired. I slowly eliminated meat as I noticed how sluggish I felt after eating it. I ate more veggies, seaweed and brown rice as I became aware of how great my body felt when eating these foods instead.

Of course it is possible to live in Japan and not be impacted by the environment. One friend was in Japan because her husband worked for the US military. They lived in an American-style house across from the American school, and shopped almost exclusively at the military base. With the abundance of pasta and Pizza Pops, after stepping inside their house it was difficult to tell that I was in Japan. Rather than losing weight in Japan, she gained weight.

Ultimately, I realized that the naturally occurring environmental factors that had helped me to be healthy and energetic in Japan were conscious choices I could make no matter where I was to create an environment that supported my whole health. I can choose to not keep those foods that steal my energy readily available in my house. I can choose to cultivate friendships with health conscious people who share my values. I can choose to walk or cycle rather than driving.

Regardless of where you live, if you are struggling with improving your health or energy, look to your environment. Instead of putting all your efforts into changing yourself, invest some time into designing an environment that will naturally move you towards your goals.

TWENTY TWO

Single vs. Family:
The Right to Choose

Family
(Kazoku)

The people you allow into your life to celebrate its joys and sorrows, and to whom you, sometimes unknowingly, entrust the power to create them.

A recent article in The Japan Times suggested that Japanese people in their 20s and 30s are delaying marriage and family due to income concerns. The article further suggested that this was a signpost of impending economic doom. I got married when I was 39 and had my first child at 41, but income (or lack thereof) was not a factor in my timing, so I couldn't help but think that young people who delay marriage and family might be influenced by reasons similar to my own. I sat down to consider all of the non-financial reasons for this trend that had influenced my decision. Here is what I came up with:

A Desire to Find Myself

By the time I was 25, a majority of my friends were married with babies in tow. At 26, three months before my own wedding, I passed up my impending trip to the altar in favor of pursuing my dream of backpacking through Asia. Crazy as it seemed to my family, I realized there were just too many things I wanted to do for and by myself that wouldn't be the same if I were married. I knew that if I didn't do these things I would end up living with regrets and "what ifs."

This desire to discover myself, follow my passions and live life without regrets landed me in Japan and kept me there for five years as I began developing and teaching the principles I now use in my coaching and consulting work. It also spurred me to leave yet another significant relationship behind in Tokyo to return to Canada and pursue the next evolution of my business.

Fear of Making the Wrong Choice

With the increasing prevalence of divorce, young people today are well aware that marriage may not be forever — and of the steep price paid by the couple (and their kids) when it isn't. In my case this led to me being much more cautious (some might have even said cynical) about falling in love. The divorce statistics provide ample evidence that marrying your high-school sweetheart is more likely to result in disaster than a lifetime of bliss. Being conscious of this puts a healthy set of brakes on the rush down the aisle fueled by youthful romanticism.

The Older You Get, the Pickier You Become

When you have a healthy fear of making the wrong choice and take the time to get to know yourself, you become more aware of what you want and less inclined to settle for anything less.

Marriage and parenthood involve sacrifices. As much as I love my husband and my son, I am the first to remind my single friends (when they are lamenting their singledom) of the many freedoms that I took for granted when I was single and childless. Coming home to an apartment that looks exactly as it did when I left? Blissful! Eating nothing but popcorn for dinner just because I feel like it? Decadence! No one to question your latest clothing purchase? Freedom! Time to just sit and daydream, write in your journal, go for a run or read a book without anyone interrupting you? Peace! The challenge with delaying marriage and family is that the longer you delay, the more difficult it becomes to give up (or at least be willing to bend on) all of the wonderful rights and freedoms of being a sovereign individual.

Young people today are increasingly aware of themselves and of the realities of marriage and family. Might it not be possible that they are choosing to remain single for the many benefits and opportunities that it offers? Perceived success as a person should not depend on marriage and family. If there were less societal pressure on people to see marriage and family as the only alternative, possibly even more people would opt to remain single and/or childless – or at least enter into relationships with a more realistic understanding of the work involved in making them work. This increased understanding of the importance of finding fulfillment as an individual, outside of a relationship, is a healthy trend – not a harbinger of economic and societal meltdown.

All that said, my reasons for delaying marriage and children to begin with are what have made my experiences of it so rewarding. My burning desire to know myself and follow my passions continues to ensure me that my husband and I are the perfect fit. Whether inspiring me, infuriating me or simply leading by example, he is always there to challenge me to live up to my potential and follow my dreams. My certainty that I made the right choice leaves me with much more energy for all of the other pursuits in my life both as an individual and as a family. Our mutual pickiness means that we don't let things boil below the surface until they blow up. We tend to call each other on our stuff as it happens and luckily, because we are not twenty, we have the maturity to handle it with grace, learn from it, and make ourselves, our relationship and our lives all the better for it.

The bottom line is that there is no one choice that is best for all. Single is not better than married (or vice versa). It's just different. Sure, you miss a significant life experience if you don't have kids, but there is also a lot that you miss out on if you do. At the end of the day, what is most important is that each person looks at their own needs, desires and dreams and honors their own right to choose.

TWENTY THREE

Red Socks and Tattoos

Transience
(Hakanai)
The true nature of pretty much everything in life.

A few years ago, I came across two very powerful metaphors, red socks and tattoos, that are still transforming my choices in life and work.

First, the socks. Red socks (or any other red item) in your laundry can stain everything pink. It doesn't matter if you have a dozen offending items or just one. The outcome is the same: pink laundry. Translating this idea to life and work, there are certain people, situations and activities that have the ability to "stain" my whole day (or week, or life) no matter how small the amount.

As I have contemplated the red socks in my life, I have realized that there are certain people with whom any amount of time I spend leaves me feeling agitated. Depending on the interaction, I might leave my encounter feeling unsettled or downright upset for a few hours to a few days. There are also certain activities that can drain my whole day, no matter how little time I spend on them. These include bookkeeping, computer maintenance and arguing with my husband.

Who are those people in your life that can ruin your whole weekend in a two-minute phone call? What are those tasks that you spend hours dreading, even if they only take a short time to do? Consider what these people and activities are truly costing you. Perhaps its time you got rid of those red socks!

Now for the tattoos. Tattoos are mostly irreversible, so it's a good idea to think pretty hard before you get one. Some decisions in life are like this. Having a child and donating a kidney come to mind, but not much else.

The majority of choices we make in life are temporary. A central tenet of Buddhism is the recognition of the transitory nature of the human experience. Nothing lasts forever. Yet to look at the amount of anxiety people cause themselves over the choices they are making in their lives, you would think that every decision is a tattoo (or a baby). Whether it is asking someone out for a date, applying to a Masters degree program, deciding to go back to your home country, starting a blog or changing the copy on your website, none of these choices are permanent. You can change your mind with relatively little consequence in the grand scheme of things.

Playing with this idea, I gave myself permission for one month to be bolder, make more mistakes, and take more risks with the understanding that I could always change my mind later. The result? I got more done in less time and had more fun doing it than I had in ages. My creativity blossomed and new ideas poured in at breakneck speed.

Even better, I discovered that these two ideas work together incredibly well. Eliminating those people, situations and activities that drained me left me with more time, energy and enthusiasm to go for it and take risks in areas that really mattered.

To experience the benefits of red socks and tattoos in your own life, I encourage you to contemplate the following two simple questions.

1. Who or what is draining my energy? Who or what do I need to eliminate completely?
2. Where do I need to stop worrying so much about the consequences and just jump in, try it out, or take a risk?

You will resist the answers that come to you at first. You will be fearful of acting on the insights they bring. But keep asking the questions. Don't worry about acting on the answers you hear immediately. Slowly, over time, your awareness will turn into action all on its own.

TWENTY FOUR

Leveraging Strengths for Success

Talents
(Sainō)
The natural gifts that energize your body, fuel your spirit and point you to your purpose in life.

Any foreigner living in Japan quickly discovers the word *jōzu*, a Japanese word that means skillful or talented. When uttering any relatively coherent Japanese phrase, kind Japanese listeners eager to encourage your linguistic brilliance often exclaim, "*jōzu desu!*" While living in Japan, I would bask in this fantasy of fluency for a few seconds before quickly denying it. I knew they would soon discover the pathetic limits of my language abilities!

Language abilities aside, understanding and embracing your legitimate strengths (or *jōzu*-ness) can go a long way towards helping you to increase your energy, manage your stress, and fast-track your career.

The first step to capitalizing on your strengths is to distinguish between the two elements of being *jōzu* that get lumped together: skill and talent. A person can develop some level of skill in almost anything they set their mind to (or are forced to do). Talents, however, exist in a person's innate ways of doing independent of their level of skill. It is possible, for example, for a person to have a natural talent for music but have very little musical skill if they have not taken any training. The secret to high energy, low stress and career success lies in focusing your energy on building skills in the areas where your natural talents and abilities lie.

Why?

You Build Skills Faster

A natural talent or ability, by definition, is an area where the fundamental competencies for being good at something already exist. A person who is naturally good at distinguishing subtle differences in colors is going to be quicker at learning things like graphic design, interior design or fashion design, all of which depend upon this ability. Learning is easier, and hence faster, in areas where you already have natural strengths.

You Build Higher Levels of Skill

Because you build skills faster in areas related to your natural talents, you enjoy learning in these areas more. This naturally leads you to spend more time building these skills, and hence to build more strength in these skill areas than in ones you do not enjoy. The more you love it, the more time you spend on it. The more time you spend on it, the better you get at it. It's that simple.

Ultimately, a focus on your strengths leads to greater success. Career and financial success are more likely in areas where you quickly and easily build skills and knowledge. Not all learning is easy, and sustaining success will require you to continuously develop your skills, even in your areas of strength and talent. If you stay in areas related to your natural abilities, developing those skills will be more fun and more energizing, leaving you with more fuel to persist through the inevitable challenges of learning.

To avoid depleting yourself on the road to success, simply remember these words from Bruce Lee: "The less effort, the faster and more powerful you will be." If you position yourself in a career where the activities required for success are intrinsically rewarding and infinitely energizing, the line between work and play gets blurred and success will feel almost effortless.

TWENTY FIVE

Embracing Winter

Winter
(Fuyu)
The season without which there could be no spring.

On January 4, 2014 we got the news: my brother had cancer. He died on February 1st, less than one month later. He was only 48 years old. As he was only a year older than me, his death caused me to question how the choices I was making might be impacting my health. It made me aware of how little time I might actually have left to do what I am here to do. I felt a strong need to do more, be more and make more of a contribution, but grief had me down for the count. I went through the motions of life and work without being there. I felt frustrated that I couldn't suddenly make myself jump into action to be a better person. Despite the thoughts racing around in my head that I had to make his death mean something for my life, I was numb.

Finally I surrendered. I gave in to the numbness. I withdrew from social engagements. I didn't follow up with clients beyond what was required. I watched lots of television. My husband took on the lion's share of parenting. I let our house be dirty. We ate lots of instant food. I tried to cry, but couldn't.

For the first time in my life I gave myself permission to not motivate myself to do anything that was in any way "good" for me. I didn't force myself to journal or meditate or even exercise to try to make myself feel better. I didn't do anything I didn't want to do or that required any unnecessary effort. Somehow, somewhere inside me, I found the courage to simply be with the emotions, to accept the heaviness, to trust the process and to have faith that it would work its way through without me having to force it.

And, slowly, it did. I went from complete numbness, to acting as if nothing had happened, to finally being able to cry. I started to be able talk to friends about it. I had days where the heaviness lifted and I felt almost normal. All along the way, I honored myself and the process, doing my best to accept where I was at and to not try to make it anything different than what it was.

The most difficult part of this was honoring my need to not talk to my mother about either her process or mine. This wouldn't have been so difficult except for the fact that she happened to be living with us at the time. She had sold her house in Calgary to move to Vancouver the September before my brother died, and had bounced between our place and my sister's place in California that fall, originally planning to find her own place in January. When we found out my brother was sick, looking for a new place for her to live naturally went to the bottom of the priority list. She ended up staying with us until July, so we lived in close quarters with each other for the first six months of the grieving process.

My mom and I are very close and I have always found it easy to be there to support her emotionally and spiritually. This time, all of that changed. I simply didn't have the energy to support her in her process while I was struggling with my own. Normally, we would have been the first person each other would go to in order to work through our thoughts and feelings, but for some reason I didn't want to talk to her about my feelings or hear about hers. I felt bad about this. Typically, I would have forced myself to check in on how she was feeling, listen to her and try to share my feelings. But somehow I knew that part of the gift in this challenge for me was to trust that others would be fine if I just stayed true to myself and surrendered to the process.

In addition to my brother passing that year, my husband, several close friends, and several clients all lost significant family members. I saw through watching them deal with grief that it was definitely possible to force yourself to keep going and resist the natural cycle that grief wanted to take you through. I also saw that resisting the cycle did not really work. It eventually caught up with them.

Going through this process reminded me of one of the things I loved most about living in Japan — the way they honor the four distinct seasons. My brother's death taught me how important it is to embrace all of the seasons and cycles of life, including death. I learned to trust that, even though winter can be scary, uncomfortable, and seem endless, spring eventually comes. I also had to learn that, just like with the Borg from Star Trek, when it comes to the winter of grief, resistance is futile.

Whether you are dealing with someone's physical death, or simply the ending of something else in your life, I encourage you to remember that it is all part of the natural cycle of life. Endings beget beginnings. Winter leads to spring. Fall must inevitably turn into winter. Each season has its own beauty, if you embrace it. To do so, simply remember that you can't control the seasons, only the amount of stress you create for yourself by trying to resist them.

TWENTY SIX

Food for Change

Food
(Shokuryou)
*That which is necessary for life, but
not sufficient for truly living.*

As a working mom, I am constantly bombarded with information about what I should be doing to be a good mother, wife and business person. I should always feed my family healthy, organic, creative meals. I should always be available to help friends and family with their trials and celebrate their triumphs. I should network, volunteer, advance my career (or grow business revenues) and, of course, I should do this all while staying fit and looking fantastic along the way. Needless to say, it is easy to feel like I will never measure up.

Most of the moms I talk to feel the same way. They are exhausted and overwhelmed by the number of areas in which they expect themselves to achieve. As food preparation is one of the main places my clients feel weighed down by expectations and self-judgment, I thought I would use it to illustrate some key principles of creating positive change in your life:

1. Set Your Own Standards

When it comes to food, as with other areas of our lives, there are many different points of view about the right way to do things. Should you be gluten-free, dairy-free, vegetarian, vegan, paleo or low carb? Yes, it is important to look to external experts for advice and research, but the best way to determine what is right for you is to look inside. Look at your beliefs and challenge them. Do you really need to create new meals from scratch every night? Do you have to eat organic all of the time? Any area where you feel a "should" slipping in, stop and ask yourself where the belief is coming from and if it is actually important for you. Replace "should" with "choose to" to set your own standards. Let go of the rest.

2. Start Where You Are

No matter what positive change you are trying to make in your life, everyone starts from a different place. If you were raised on meat and potatoes, white bread, fast food and very few veggies, and you have been feeding your family this way for years, it can be hard to make changes. It feels like you need to start over completely, invest huge amounts of time and give up all of the comfort foods you love. This does not need to be the case. You can start by simply substituting whole grain bread for white bread or adding raw veggies and hummus to every meal. If you feel exhausted from trying to keep up with cooking "proper" meals and find yourself resorting to fast food more often than you would like, your path to positive change might involve cooking larger amounts when you do cook so that you can freeze one or two meals for a future date. Acknowledge your starting point and work from there.

3. Avoid Intention Overload

Every change we make takes energy, so it is important not to try to change too many things at once or you will not have the energy to see any of them through. Pick one area of your life that you most want to optimize and work on that. If it is eating more healthfully, work on that. If exercising more feels like it would have a big payoff, put all of your efforts toward creating change in that area. If getting ahead at work is what you are most excited about, set your goals, develop a plan and execute it. Let go of the other things you want and trust that you will get to them later. If you focus on the one area that feels most important, it will have spillover benefits into your other goals. Once success in a key area is achieved, you might realize that you really don't care about the other goals and choose to leave them undone.

4. Keep It Simple

Don't try cooking in ways that require you to completely change the taste-buds of you and your family. Start with staples that you know and love. Find how many ways you can to add dark leafy greens to old favorites. I puree kale with veggie broth and combine that with ground beef or turkey when I make shepherd's pie. I also use a combination of mashed sweet potatoes and cauliflower instead of white potatoes. Those two small changes have turned a family favorite comfort food into a meal that also packs a hefty nutritious punch.

5. Create Routines

Just as you are more likely to exercise if you have a consistent routine, you will find it easier to eat healthfully if you create streamlined routines for meeting the nutrition needs of your family. Introducing fruit shakes for weekday breakfasts is one example of a new healthy routine that can be easily implemented. A big blender, some protein powder and some frozen fruit is all you need to make a healthy breakfast for your family in a matter of minutes. Another simple routine that goes a long way towards healthier eating is to chop up a big tub of veggies and keep it in the fridge ready to snack on. I do mine every Sunday and always have plenty of hummus on hand to go with it. My son gets a plate of veggies and hummus to munch on for his snack each day when he gets his half hour of daily screen time while I am making dinner.

6. Ask For Help

Making yourself 100% responsible for changes that require buy-in from others is bound to zap your energy. If you want to make changes that everyone will benefit from, get input from your family on what they want and where they can contribute. From a very young age in my family, each family member was responsible for cooking one meal per week. My youngest sister often made hot dogs or spaghetti when she was young, but as we all got older and more skilled, we looked forward to our cooking day to try out new recipes on each other.

7. Let Go

One of the frequent complaints I hear from my female clients is that their spouses or children don't help out as much as they would like. In some instances these clients realized that they had contributed to the problem by not being willing to let go of anything until someone else picked it up. Imagine someone running as fast as they can with a heavy backpack and complaining that no one else will carry it for them. You have to slow down and take off the pack so someone else can pick it up! Remember: you will likely need to leave that pack sitting there much longer than you would like to before someone else figures out they need to pick it up. You may even need to ask them to do it if they don't figure it out on their own. Ultimately, most of my clients are surprised to discover that their family will actually help out if they slow down and wait for them to do it at their own pace.

8. Be Patient With Yourself

There will be false starts. You will fall off the wagon. Don't expect change to happen too quickly. A good plan involves small changes over long periods of time. Month one might involve keeping chopped veggies in the fridge at all times. Month two you develop the habit of cooking one meal a week that you freeze something for a future meal. Month three might be replacing white bread with whole wheat. Month four you introduce one new recipe each week, or one new recipe per month for a year. Keep goals small and focus on building sustainable habits instead of quick results and you will be more likely to succeed.

No matter what gender you are, learning to survive and thrive requires looking at the roles you believe you are supposed to fill, re-thinking them and designing them to fit you and your life. Whether you want to change food, fitness, career, relationships or parenting, I hope that the above principles inspire you to remember that sustainable change must be based on knowing who you are, what you want and what can realistically be expected of any human being.

TWENTY SEVEN

Barriers to Work You Love

Work
(Shigoto)
Done wrong, its a living - done right, its your life.

Over my 25 years of coaching people to create careers that align with their passions, I have encountered dozens of ways that people block themselves and the process. After a recent session with one of my clients in Asia, I recognized that the following five are the most common:

1. Competition and the Need for Approval

Humans have natural needs for safety, belonging, love, power, control and achievement. While these needs must be addressed, allowing them to be the driving force behind your actions and decisions thwarts your ability to meet higher level needs for purpose, passion, alignment, balance, creativity and inspiration. If your career choices are heavily influenced by the desire to compete with friends, please family or look good to colleagues, you are falling prey to this limitation. Clarifying core passions like values, strengths and purpose will provide a foundation to guide your choices with your internal compass instead of allowing yourself to be buffeted by the prevailing winds.

2. Thinking You Missed the Boat

"I wish I would have stuck with it, but..."
"If only I had..." "I'm too old to..."
"All of my colleagues are already...."

In the first few sessions of our work together, my client frequently expressed versions of the above limiting beliefs regarding her passion for dance and yoga. As we progressed through examining all of her passions, however, it became clear to me that she had not "missed the boat." She had simply chosen not to get on previous boats because they didn't fit all of her passions, particularly the intellectual rigor and stimulation that her other interests held for her. When she recognized that she had not made a mistake and missed an opportunity, but rather that her internal passions had been guiding her all along, it eliminated her self-doubt, and increased her confidence for taking the next steps to make her passions into her livelihood. I must add that this client was only 30!

I wish I could say that it is unusual for me to hear people talking about "missing the boat" at such a young age. Media loves to make lists like the "Top 30 Under 30," and celebrate young people who have "made it." While they do so precisely because these people are the exception to the rule, the volume of these kinds of images that we are exposed to creates the impression that if you haven't made it by 35, you're washed up.

This limiting belief hits other areas like relationships as well. When I arrived in Japan after traveling Asia, I was 26 and single. I quickly learned that there was a special Japanese word to describe me: "Christmas cake." Huh? Apparently, the 26th is the day after which Christmas cake is no good to eat, and 26 is the age after which a young woman is no longer good to marry. Suffice it to say, no matter what culture you come from, the glorification of youth makes this belief common.

Despite it's prevalence, this "too late" belief is a complete fallacy, regardless of whether you are 30 or 70. I have had the privilege of knowing people who changed their career trajectory in their 30s, those who reinvented themselves in their 50s and those who didn't find their true purpose until their 70s.

3. Believing It's Not Possible

The most common subset of this limiting belief is the idea that you can't make money doing what you love. This limitation is especially prevalent in those who have talents and interests that lie in creative areas like the arts, but it can include any belief that starts with "Everyone knows that..." These beliefs are founded on being practical, realistic, and buying into common stereotypes. Practicality is not a bad thing, but it causes you to limit options prematurely in the career visioning process.

4. Letting Strategy Dictate Vision

Human beings are great natural strategists. If a person in the career visioning stage can't immediately envision the strategy to reach their vision, they discard the vision. Taken to it's natural end, this leaves the person with a career vision that they feel confident they can achieve. Isn't that a good thing?

Unfortunately, no. An achievable vision and a satisfying one are not always the same thing. Here's why: Imagine your big dream is to travel around the world for a year, but you can't figure out how you would find the time and money to do it. You do your budget, consider your holiday allotment from your job, and decide that a realistic goal is to take two weeks each year to travel somewhere in North America by car. The challenge is that, while this is a realistic goal, it is highly unlikely that these smaller local trips are going to provide you with the fulfillment of your real dream – a one-year sabbatical traveling to exotic places around the world.

A huge part of my work with clients involves keeping them out of strategy mode so that they can allow themselves to see what they really want. Once they identify what they really want, it is time to work on strategy. The good news about this is that even downsized goals take time and effort to achieve. When a person is working towards a vision that truly excites and inspires them, they are far more likely to persist long enough to achieve it. If you have a history of not following through on career goals, there is a good chance that your goals were based on what you felt was realistic to achieve vs. what was truly inspiring to you.

5. The Career Doesn't Exist Yet

Our society by and large still works from the mindset of "finding" a job. This mindset assumes that the job, career or business already exists to be found. The new reality is that the world of work is in major flux. Many types of work are becoming obsolete and many others are being created. Web designer jobs, for example, were non-existent several decades ago, as were all of the entrepreneurial and employment opportunities that have exploded with the advent of the Internet. There is a good chance that the work you are meant to do is in an industry that needs to be created, and isn't simply waiting to be found.

At the end of the day, identifying and achieving a career vision that delivers on all of your dreams requires being mindful of these beliefs, but that is not enough. It also requires having the courage and creativity to get and stay connected with the internal passion that inspires commitment — not just for the moment, but for a lifetime.

TWENTY EIGHT

Out With the Old

Purification
(Kiyome)
*Cleansing yourself of the past to create new
energy with which to face the future.*

Japanese year-end traditions are one of the many things about
Japan that have continued to play a big part in my life and work
since I returned to Canada more than a decade ago. I don't
eat the traditional foods, and I prefer to save my major floor
cleaning and waxing for spring when I can leave the windows
open to air things out, but I do observe two Japanese traditions:
ōsōji (year end cleaning) and *bonenkai* (the "forget the year"
celebration) at home and at work.

As *ōsōji* is about purifying yourself and preparing to enter
the new year literally "free and clean," I like to concentrate
on cleaning out both the physical and mental clutter that has
claimed my energy throughout the year. At home this means a
good purging of the clothing in my drawers and closets, being

as brutal as I can about letting go of any items that haven't seen the light of day in the past year.

I also use this time to take stock of my personal relationships, look at which ones need to be mended and determine if any need to be let go. While this may sound a bit harsh, after decades of practicing this habit I can honestly say that all of my personal relationships are well worth keeping. This is not to say that they are without their challenges, but they do all contribute significantly to my happiness, growth, success and overall wellbeing. My rule for determining which relationships are worth keeping, nurturing and mending is whether that relationship gives more to me than it takes. (Hint: You can't do this evaluation with a balance sheet, you need to do it with your heart. Externally it can look like you are giving more, but you might be receiving bountifully in less visible ways such as the joy and energy it gives you to be of service to others in ways that use your strengths and fulfill your purpose.)

At work we apply this tradition to both ourselves and our clients. Our annual strategic planning process begins in October with taking stock of the previous year, reviewing progress and reordering priorities based on what we want to be sure to complete in the final quarter. While we like to be done most of our own key projects by mid-November so we can focus on the influx of clients that need help with their strategic plans, December still brings a strong drive to finish off any last things dragging on our own lists. Our lists of projects that need completion is often longer than our time will allow, so we use the following questions to decide which to complete, which to roll over into the coming year and which to delete altogether:

- How long has this project/task been on our plate? How close is it to completion? How badly do I want to NOT put it on my strategic plan or to-do list next year (or ever again!)?

- What is the potential positive impact its completion will have on me, my team, the business, or our client? (How much time/energy/resources will its completion free up? What will completing this allow us to move forward on?)

- What are the potential consequences if we just let it go? What would happen if we decided to never complete it and deleted it altogether? A great example of this is the cabinets of paper files I keep for research when developing training sessions. We had slotted these to be scanned by our assistant in our drive to take our office paperless. When I realized that I had not looked at 75% of the contents of those cabinets in several years, and that all of that information (and more) was readily available on the Internet I knew it was time to purge. I threw most of it away, saving my assistant days of work.

Finally, to celebrate all of our accomplishments and say goodbye to the troubles and challenges of the past year, we have started our own *bonenkai* tradition. As my partner and I are not big drinkers, rather than drowning our memories in champagne, we bathe and massage them away with a relaxing day at the spa. No point ruining all that purity with a wicked hangover!

TWENTY NINE

Don't Retire, Re-Inspire!

Retirement
(Taishoku)
*Something you will lose the desire to do once
you connect with your purpose.*

By the time most people hit 40, they have begun putting aside money for their retirement. Unfortunately, they have put little time or effort into the following five factors that are key determinants of thriving as they approach and enter into the retirement phase of their life.

1. Create a Compelling Vision for Your Future

For all too many people — especially those who spent their careers living for the weekend — a retirement vision consists solely of the absence of work. Unfortunately, permanent weekends of endless shopping, golf, gardening, and TV quickly lose their appeal. Retirement is not a time to give up on setting goals.

It is a time to get better at identifying the goals that really excite you now that you are not constrained by the need to work.

2. Connect With Your Purpose

Without the need to pay the bills, what would make you excited to get up each morning? It may come as a surprise to know that it is not the pursuit of unending leisure activities that provides thriving retirees with a source of boundless energy and enthusiasm. Research shows that people of any age can tap into huge stores of vitality when they connect with a purpose beyond their own preservation, profit or pleasure.

3. Make a Plan

Your vision and purpose should determine your financial plan, not the other way around. A concrete sense of what you are saving for makes it easier to set the money aside, but it also informs the amount. The amount you need to save will vary greatly depending on whether your "happy place" consists of 5-star world travel or picnics in the park with your grandkids who live down the block. Don't even attempt to figure this out on your own. Interview three to five financial professionals, including at least one fee-for-service investment planner, one fee-for-service money coach and one accountant (preferably a tax and estate planning specialist) before deciding who you are going to have guide you in growing your financial portfolio.

4. Create Structure

As much as people might hate the forced routine of their job, that rhythm serves them well in being able to get things done. Experiencing a sense of accomplishment and productivity on a regular basis is a very core human need that goes unmet in retirement once the structure of a job disappears. Many of my clients need help establishing new structures and routines that are more suited to their natural style so that they can feel both productive and retired at the same time. One technique that works well is to designate certain days of the week "productivity" days to focus on their goals, and others "free" days to go with the flow and do what they want.

5. Be Accountable

When you no longer have a boss or co-workers to be accountable to, who makes you follow through on your commitments? Hiring a professional coach is a great way to help you create workable plans for achieving your goals and ensure that you follow through, but making firm commitments with a friend or spouse can work as well. Be cautious though: friends and family may either let you off the hook too easily or pressure you into doing things their way rather than your own.

6. Strengthen Your Relationships

There is an abundance of research available that links mental, physical and emotional health at every age to the strength of one's social networks. This is not about how many friends you have on Facebook. It is about the depth of the real human connections and support networks you have that encourage you to be your authentic self and pursue your dreams. Unfortunately this can also require having the courage to let go of the relationships that don't strengthen you. It is better to have a few relationships that truly energize you than lots of relationships that don't add real value to your life.

The great thing about the above ideas is that they are keys to fulfillment no matter what your age or stage of life. Those who are fulfilled in retirement also tend to have been most fulfilled in their careers because they adhered to the above principles. Always remember that the true key to success is not only having the discipline to save for your future, but the courage to turn down opportunities that only pay well in favor of those that leave you feeling good about yourself at the end of the day.

THIRTY

Energize Your Life and Work

Energy
(Ki)
Your most valuable commodity: learn to manage it well.

In Japanese, the phrases *"(O)genki desu ka"* and *"Genki desu"* are used to express the common sentiments "How are you?" and "I am fine." However, since genki is translated as not just "okay" or "fine" but as "healthy, happy, energetic, lively and enthusiastic," these phrases actually have a much more inspiring undertone. What you are really being asked is "Are you happy, healthy, energetic and enthusiastic?" So, in order to legitimately respond "Genki desu," you need to actually be happy, healthy and energetic.

I love this greeting because I have always felt more energetic upon declaring myself "genki." This supports the many scientific studies proving the power our words have to influence our state of being.

To help you get *genki*, here are my top tips for getting and staying energized all day long.

Get More Sleep

I know. You want to do it all. You want to work, travel, sleep, exercise, study and still have time to spend with your family. Cutting back on sleep seems like the easiest way to find yourself another few hours to do all those things you want to do. Big mistake! Your brain uses sleep to restore optimum physical, mental and emotional functioning. Without proper sleep, your productivity, creativity, mental sharpness, emotional balance and physical vitality diminishes. If you have a hard time getting out of bed in the morning, use caffeine and sugar to perk yourself up, get sleepy in meetings or fall asleep easily while watching TV, you are sleep deprived. Most adults need between 7.5 and 9 hours per night. Most get only 6-7. That extra hour or two can be the deciding factor between thriving and just surviving.

Get Enough Exercise

Notice that I didn't say get more exercise. More is not always better. Anyone who has suffered from the post-workout stiffness and fatigue of an overzealous workout gets this. The key to understanding how much exercise is enough for you to achieve your energy (or weight and fitness) goals with least effort is the minimum effective dose (MED). This is the smallest dose that will produce a desired outcome.

The MED for boiling water is 100°C. Anything beyond that is overkill. Tim Ferriss, author of The 4 Hour Body, shows that the MED for building muscles anywhere you want them is just 80 seconds of lifting 20lbs daily, not hours of pumping metal at the gym. My exercise MED for optimum energy is a 15 minute run in nature at least 5 days/week. Whether by research or personal experimentation, the MED is the key to more energy (and results) with less effort in every area of your life.

Use Coffee Strategically

No, I am not going to tell you to stop drinking coffee. I love my java too much for that! And I am not going to tell you that it is bad for you. The verdict is still out on that, and I know which side I am hoping for. I am going to tell you how it actually works so that you can understand how to use it more strategically to boost energy.

Based on *Buzz: The Science and Lore of Alcohol and Caffeine* by Stephen Braun, caffeine itself doesn't perk you up. It just blocks the receptors that make you feel sleepy, giving other happy chemicals like dopamine free reign to work their magic for a while. Unfortunately, within a week of regular caffeine consumption, humans become tolerant of their daily dose(s) to the point where they don't feel any benefit.

To restore caffeine to a functional (and pleasurable) role in your energy management repertoire, you need to "dry out" for at least several days between each use. This is long enough to trigger the headaches, fatigue, irritability and other nasty symptoms that we caffeine junkies experience. However, it's worth it in order to be able to use caffeine more strategically for energy enhancement in your real times of need.

Sometimes, our caffeine habits are entwined with other needs. While nursing your caffeine headache, it might be a good time to think about the situations and feelings that trigger these cravings. This could help you discover chronic energy leaks that can save you tons of time and energy.

The above three tips can do wonders for ramping up your physical energy. Equally important, however, is paying attention to your mental, emotional and spiritual energy. The next chapter provides more strategies for ramping up your emotional and spiritual energy while also learning to better manage stress.

THIRTY ONE

Stressed in the City

Stress
(Omoni)

The result of a lack of clarity about who you are,
or a lack of alignment between who you are and
the circumstances in your life or work.

Six months after returning to Canada following a five year sojourn working in Japan, I had a moment of enlightenment regarding how stressful it is to be immersed in an environment where doing even the most basic things does not come naturally to you.

I was on my way to the bank when I noticed that I was rehearsing in my head what I was going to say to the teller — in English! After having a good laugh at myself, it dawned on me that mentally rehearsing unfamiliar interactions in Japanese had become a normal part of my everyday life. The recognition that I no longer needed to engage in this habit was a huge relief.

This got me thinking about sources of stress, and whether the solutions that most experts tout (exercise, meditation, journaling, etc.) are really effective. I had engaged in these stress management behaviors while living in Japan on a regular basis and they had helped at first, but after awhile the stress of living in an environment that was so unnatural to me built up to the point that the only thing that would manage it was leaving.

This points to the fact that there is a deeper source of stress in most people's lives: a lack of alignment between who they are and the life circumstances they find themselves in. Rather than trying to add in one more thing to your overloaded schedule, consider the following four opportunities to eliminate stress by realigning your life and work with your true self.

1. Learn to Leverage Your Strengths

If your energy is depleted, you don't have any resources available to combat stress, so the first step in combating stress is to find a way to fill your tank. Spending time each day using and developing your preferred strengths is a great start.

Doing what you love is a key source of energy. Think of that good tired feeling you get after spending a day doing something you really love. While you might be physically or even mentally tired, you feel emotionally and spiritually energized.

To really leverage your strengths, it is important to differentiate between strengths and skills. Anyone can develop skill through repetition and necessity. Your natural strengths, however, will stand out from those areas where you are simply skilled due to the following two characteristics:

1. You will be energized by performing these activities and/ or learning about these subjects (regardless of how skilled/ knowledgeable you are at them).

2. You will learn more quickly and develop higher levels of expertise in areas that are aligned with your natural strengths.

Doing things you don't like (even if you are skilled at them) creates distress and diminishes your energy. Doing things you love (even if you aren't that skilled yet) creates eustress (positive stress) and actually gives you energy. Even a few hours spent bookkeeping will exhaust me, but a 16 hour day spent training or coaching will leave me with that energized, "good tired" feeling as I fall happily into bed at night.

To boost your energy and tap into this "good tired" natural immunization against stress, consider the following:

- Do you enjoy learning about music, art, business or the latest technology? Put this source of energy to good use in your teaching by crafting it into games and learning activities for your students. Offer to share this passion with your colleagues by doing a lunch-and-learn training session for them at work.

- Do you prefer working with a group more than on your own in certain phases of a project? Enlist a team to work with you at the point in projects where you usually find your energy flagging and your stress increasing.

- Are you in sales? How can you bring your talent for connecting people or your passion for research to the forefront to build stronger relationships with your customers?

- Are you a leader in a large organization? The areas of your job that are most energizing for you point to your greatest opportunities for both contributing to the organization and reducing your own stress. Identify the aspects of your role that drain you. Then either systematize or delegate them so you can focus on doing what you do best.

2. Close Your Integrity Gaps

The next strategy to immunize yourself against stress involves identifying and closing your integrity gaps.

Integrity gaps exist whenever your actions are not in alignment with your most deeply held values, principles and beliefs. Ever had that tight feeling in the pit of your stomach as a result of something you have said or done (or maybe something you witnessed someone else say or do)? That is a symptom of an integrity gap.

Have you ever gone along with your friends on something you didn't want to do, agreed with the boss's opinion for the sole purpose of climbing the corporate ladder or failed to stand up for yourself when you were treated poorly? You might have been conscious of how and why you compromised yourself in the moment, but more often than not these small "integrity gaps" went unnoticed on a conscious level. The problem is that each of these little compromises drains your energy.

The easiest way to understand how this works is to think of the gas tank of a car. Each instance of misalignment between your actions and your values creates a small hole in the gas tank. Each hole may only be the size of a pin prick, but it still leaks gas from the tank. If such behavior is repeated over time, the small holes become larger and eventually gas is leaking out of your tank faster than it can be put in. In short, the more your daily behavior is out of alignment with your values, principles and beliefs, the more stress you will feel.

You don't need to move to a foreign country to know how stressful it can be to function in a foreign culture. Every organization has its own distinct culture as well. If the company you work for operates on very different values, principles and beliefs than the ones that you feel aligned with, you are going to feel the same type of stress that you would living in a foreign country. Working in a culture that is not naturally aligned with your values forces you to invest extra energy evaluating your actions and decisions to determine how they will be received, the negative consequences they might create and the best way to get the results you desire.

But just as the person living in a foreign country can't change that culture, it is very difficult, if not impossible, to change the culture of a business (unless you are the owner or CEO). My clients in Japan often chose to patch up their Japan-related integrity gaps by returning to their home country. In the same way, my clients with workplace culture related integrity gaps usually choose to cut their losses and look for a place to work that is more aligned with their values.

Unfortunately, this solution will only relieve your stress temporarily. Everyone experiences integrity gaps on a daily basis, no matter where they live or work. There are two reasons for this:

1. You are not consciously aware of your values, beliefs and principles, or the promises you have made to yourself about what you want to stand for and how you want to be. If you aren't consciously aware you have made a promise, then it is much more likely that you will break that promise.

2. Lower level needs are taking precedence. Your inner values compass gets put on the back burner when basic needs for safety, love and self-esteem feel threatened. You are less likely to resist the white lie if your job is on the line or you are trying to impress your date.

The solution? Spend some time thinking about the values and principles that you want to use as the foundation for your actions and decisions. Then look at all areas of your life and identify where the major misalignments are. Don't try to tackle them all at once. Pick the one that is most draining your energy and make a plan to be more aligned with your values and less driven by your needs. If that feels too daunting, start with the easiest one first.

Whether you take big leaps or baby steps in closing these integrity gaps, the end result will be less stress, more energy and a greater sense of wellbeing.

3. Tap Into the Power of Purpose

The third way to boost energy and immunize yourself against stress it to connect with your purpose. Research shows that individuals with a clear sense of purpose and the ability to find meaning in both positive and negative events are more resilient in times of crisis.

Why is this?

From a very young age we begin to ask why. These early questions stem from the inherent knowledge that everything in life has meaning and purpose. In nature, everything has a purpose. Every plant, animal, insect, stream, and natural process has some specific contribution to make to the whole.

Everything is interconnected. Everything is important. Everything has its own special purpose.

Unfortunately, as we grow older, we are trained to stop asking why and to just do as we are told. While this might support short-term survival, it is a major barrier to our ability to thrive. Thriving requires that we cultivate our ability to find meaning and purpose in everything in life.

Just as each species has a unique niche and an environment where they function best, so does each person. If you take an insect or animal out of its indigenous environment, you run the risk of upsetting the balance both in the new environment and in the old one. Discovering purpose and seeking meaning in all events in your life directs you to the niche where you are best able to thrive. This supports the optimal health of the whole system. It also explains why aligning with your purpose is critical for building resilience in the face of crisis.

To identify your own unique purpose, begin by looking at the contributions you already make in your life and work. What do you do to make a difference to your family, your friends, your workplace or your community? Think about the talents and strengths you have and how you naturally use them in a way that serves others. Think about your values, the choices you make and your natural ways of being. Consider how these contribute to those around you.

The next step is to look at the needs you see. Not everyone sees the same needs. The needs you see and your level of passion for them are related to the abilities, talents and resources you have access to that can address those needs. When you are giving to others in ways that align with your purpose, it is more likely to energize you than stress you out.

4. Right-Size Your Vision

The final element that is at the root of stress for many successful people is their vision.

The first pitfall is not having a vision at all. Having no vision for your life and work causes stress because you have nothing to work towards, nothing to look forward to and nothing to challenge yourself to achieve. Successful people experience this once they have reached a major career or life goal. They almost burn themselves out to achieve the goal, coast for awhile to enjoy their accomplishment, and then, one day wake up to realize that they have a different kind of stress: the stress of being stuck in the rinse-and-repeat rat race of doing more of the same each day.

The second source of stress is a vision that is too small. Most people limit their visions based on what they think they can realistically achieve. Unfortunately visions that are too realistic don't light a fire under your butt to start taking action right away. This fuels procrastination, which in turn creates the stress that comes from knowing that you are not taking action to move towards your vision.

Another reason small visions cause stress is that most people don't achieve everything they set out to do. From large-scale disasters to small scale surprises, there are always unforeseen factors that get in the way of going as far and as fast as you would like. To get around this pitfall take a lesson from the most successful businesses – over-design. If you want to sell 1000 units/month, design a strategy to sell 2000. You will have to think very differently to sell and deliver on 2000 units. The great news is that if you shoot for 2000, you can still fail by 50% and achieve your original vision of 1000 units! Stretching beyond the limits of what you think is possible forces you to challenge the old thinking patterns that are limiting your success. Hint: many of the thinking patterns responsible for your current success are the same ones that are limiting your ability to get to the next level.

A compelling vision is energizing in and of itself, but it also provides focus and direction that prevents you from wasting energy pursuing too many different vectors. Just like you can eat too many sweets, you can overload yourself with work opportunities, hobbies and social activities. When your vision is clear, it becomes easier to tell which of the many good things you are being offered are really and truly good for you.

If you are feeling stressed, by all means get some exercise, meditate, get enough sleep and take concrete actions to look after your physical body. Just don't forget that none of these will address the root cause of your stress: the misalignment between who you really want to be and the current circumstances of your life. When you combine the physical energy tips from the previous chapter with these techniques for ramping up your mental, emotional and spiritual energy, you will ultimately develop the ability to stay *genki* from dawn to dusk.

THIRTY TWO

The Way of the Shokunin

Master
(Sensei)

*A person who, despite being at the top of their craft,
is still excited by how much there is to learn.*

Jiro Ono is a famous Tokyo sushi chef who, at 85, has no intentions of retiring until he is incapable of showing up to work. His work brings so much meaning, purpose and joy to his life that he cannot imagine life without it. To him, work is not a paycheque. It is a privilege. As the first sushi restaurant to be awarded a three Michelin star rating, he is also a recognized master in his field.

After watching Jiro Dreams of Sushi, the documentary chronicling Jiro's approach to life and work, I felt that Jiro's story provided key insights into what it takes to achieve mastery in any profession. *Shokunin*, which can be roughly translated to a master craftsman or artisan, implies a mindset that makes it possible to fill your work with joy, vitality, and purpose no matter what it may be.

Mastering Mindfulness

Jiro is so committed to providing the perfect experience for his clients that he adjusts the size of the sushi to the size of the patron, and the placement on their plate according to whether they are right- or left-handed. Details matter. They are the difference between going through the motions and really caring. This benefits the customer, but it also benefits the worker. Being mindful of the details keeps you fully engaged in your work. It brings the priceless feeling of a job well done and potential realized.

Understanding Enough

Size does matter, but bigger isn't always better. Jiro's restaurant seats only 11 people. He could have capitalized on his fame with a larger restaurant, but that would have prevented him from giving the kind of service and the quality of product that he is famous for.

Japanese culture is full of examples that less is often more. Jiro only serves sushi. He recognizes that excellence comes from the ability and the courage to focus. This is true not only for the size of your business and the number of your products, but for your lifestyle and work. Climbing the career ladder may not bring you more joy than working every day in a job you love. A small condo might bring you more contentment than a big house. Right-size your life based on your own values rather than on external standards or expectations.

Challenge, Change and Creativity

Jiro literally dreams of sushi — both how to improve his skills and how to exceed each customer's expectations. He experiments constantly, looking for ways to make small improvements as well as being willing to try something completely different. Success and fulfillment in any field require these same abilities.

Passion, Purpose and Personal Responsibility

Jiro believes that a person has only two choices: to fall in love with their work or to find new work. Would he have found the same sense of calling as a plumber, salesman, teacher or tailor? I suspect he could have, but if he didn't he would have moved on to something else until he did. This attitude differentiates the true *shokunin* from the mere seeker.

The most dangerous belief of the seekers is that the successful business owner, executive, artist or guru who also loves her work somehow "got lucky" to find that perfect career. This belief is dangerous because it reinforces two myths about finding work you love: 1) that there is only one career where you can find both passion and fulfillment; and 2) that you have to get lucky to find it.

Assuming that ideal work must be stumbled upon rather than created propagates a lack of commitment and personal responsibility. This is the antithesis of the *shokunin* mindset.

Every person I have studied and worked with over the last two decades that has "found" their passion demonstrates a common skill and mindset: they took personal responsibility for actively creating passion and artistry in every job they had. Whether they were a bus driver, a clerk at 7-11, or a leading executive, they brought their full passion, commitment and creativity to whatever role they were in. While many of these success stories might also attribute their success and fulfillment to luck, their stories reveal the truth: it was their commitment to fulfilling their potential in every job they had that propelled them along.

To adopt the *shokunin* mindset and achieve fulfillment in whatever you choose, remember that mastery is an ongoing journey. You create it rather than searching for it by committing to constantly craft your spirit, challenge your creativity, make a difference, and tap into the vitality and purpose that comes from aiming for nothing less than your best in all you do.

THIRTY THREE

Reinventing Yourself

Transformation
(Henka)
The constant reinvention that characterizes an authentic life.

Like many accomplished professionals, you may have embarked upon your career path for reasons that have little to do with your true passions. I have had numerous clients who became accountants, doctors or lawyers due to family values or pressure. Other clients have simply fallen into their career because of the first job they happened upon after university.

The challenge is this. If your career path has been determined by anything other than an understanding of your true talents, interests and passions, chances are your enjoyment of your work is limited. Spending a majority of your time doing things you don't enjoy is a surefire recipe for low energy, stress and mediocrity. Doing what you love, on the other hand, not only leads to excellence, success and happiness; it is the ultimate source of renewable and sustainable energy on a personal level.

For many of the people I worked with while living in Japan, it offered the perfect opportunity to break free from doing what they had always done. Not only were they away from old influences, they were surrounded by new ones. This allowed (and even forced) them to make new choices about who and how they wanted to be. Fortunately, moving to a foreign country is not necessary to the process of reinvention. Here's how to break free of old patterns and revitalize your life and work, no matter where you live:

Identify Influences

How much has your current path/personality been influenced by your true talents, interests and passions vs. the opinions of others? No need for judgment or regret. Simply recognize what is and choose to steer by your own inner compass from now on.

Cultivate Your Passions

Four key passions are required to recalibrate your internal compass and ensure that your next incarnation is more aligned with your true self — your values, talents, purpose and vision. Books are helpful, but a good career coach is invaluable for synthesizing your unique combination of passions and removing the limiting beliefs that have prevented you from seeing and following your passions before now.

Explore Your Whims

Don't worry if the things that interest you aren't practical. While none of your explorations may turn into a viable career, they are guaranteed to produce invaluable knowledge about your own style, strengths and purpose.

Pay Attention and Take Action!

My passion for cycle-touring was sparked in Japan when I overheard a couple in my favorite coffee shop planning their cycling trip to France. The next day I went out, bought a bike and began planning my first cycling trip. While not related to my work, this hobby remains an incredible source of aliveness for me to this day.

Be Willing to Let Go

When I first arrived in Japan, I had to consciously let go of my corporate identity and give myself permission to explore activities like *aikido, ikebana, shiatsu* massage, meditation, and *taiko* drumming for their own intrinsic value.

Listen to What Calls You Back

By allowing myself a full year to explore alternate personal and career identities, I had more trust in the vision that began calling me back to certain aspects of my past work in new and exciting ways.

While you may fear that the reinvention process will require completely starting over, this is seldom the case. It simply requires the willingness to entertain a fresh perspective on the foundations that have always been part of how you thrive in life and work. The risks of trying are few, the costs of staying stuck are high, and the ultimate reward is a life you love. What have you got to lose?

THIRTY FOUR

Conscious Choices

Trust
(Shinrai)

The firm belief in the reliability, truth, ability or strength of someone or something, without which faith, hope, magic and miracles are not possible.

One day, a Japanese university student came running to the temple of a Zen master crying, "Master, master, the water pipes in my apartment broke and the whole *tatami* floor is flooded, isn't it terrible?" The master simply smiled and replied "Good thing, bad thing, who knows?"

The next day, the student again came running to the master. "Isn't it wonderful master," he said "A fire broke out in the apartment next to mine last night, but because of the flood, my apartment didn't catch fire. And I'm getting new *tatami* to replace the other ones which were old and dirty anyway. Isn't it wonderful?" The master simply nodded again and said "Good thing, bad thing, who knows?"

Later that week, the student returned again to the master. "Oh master, its so unfair," said he, "My neighbor got enough money to replace all his belongings and they have moved him to a great new apartment that is twice the size of mine. Isn't it terrible?" And of course, the master only smiled and replied "Good thing, bad thing, who knows?"

The following day there was an earthquake. The ex-neighbor's new apartment was next to a huge skyscraper that collapsed on his building and killed everyone in it.

The moral of the story? You can never know the ultimate consequences of any one event in your life. This is true, not only of the things that happen to us, but also of the choices that we make — the things that we supposedly have some control over.

Take the example of choosing to stay in a job you don't like for an extra year in order to save money to have some security while you make the transition to a different field. Some of the consequences of your choices can be predicted. If you choose to stay, having a clear reason for doing so (such as a specific goal you are working towards) will help you to explain another year of experience that is not related to your chosen field. You can control how much you benefit from staying at your old job with conscious planning and being aware of opportunities to take on additional responsibilities that would fit in with your long term career and life goals.

Of course, there are also consequences of your choice to stay which you can not predict. Maybe this is the year that you will meet the man/woman of your dreams on a business trip and you will end up moving to a different country. Years from now, when you are set up in a European village with two kids and your own restaurant business, you may look back on this seemingly minor choice to stay another year as a pivotal one.

It is this lack of knowledge about and control over consequences that can make such choices a stressful part of life. What do you do when faced with a major decision? Do you obsess, agonize, analyze, avoid, or become apathetic? Or do you calmly gather the facts, spend time in quiet contemplation, seek input from valued friends and work at listening to what your instincts are telling you? Unfortunately, most people choose some combination of the first set of methods, all of which add to the stress of making such choices.

Why do people stress so much about making choices? Because they fear making a mistake. The stress that you feel when making a choice is in direct proportion to the amount of ego you have invested in getting it right. Do you fear others disapproving of your choices and thinking you stupid? Do you fear looking foolish for changing your mind? These fears are real. You might look foolish to others for changing your mind. They might not agree with your decisions and think them stupid. But what could be more foolish than sticking with a course of action you know is not right for you just to avoid a bit of embarrassment?

While I don't really believe in mistakes, (everything in life has its lessons) and I haven't made a choice I regret in ages, I do believe that it is possible to make bad choices. Bad choices are based on fear rather than faith. Bad choices are founded on values and principles that are not your own. In short, bad choices are based on seeking approval from others rather than following your own internal sense of what is right for you.

To start making good choices ask yourself these questions:

- Is this choice based on fear or on faith?
- Is this potential choice based on approval from others?

- Which option is based on what I would really like to do if only the circumstances were right?
- What have I learned from the current situation?
- What would I still like to learn or do?
- Can I do this more easily anywhere else?
- If so, what would I gain from doing it here?

Finally, remember the Zen story above and remind yourself that you have no way of knowing what is around the corner, and what amazing directions your life will take as a result of your decision to turn right or left. Stop trying to control and predict the consequences of your choices. Instead, practice living in the excitement, joy and mystery of watching the results of your choices unfold as you live them.

THIRTY FIVE

How to Know When It's Time to Go

Ending
(Ketsumatsu)
The process that unites the past and the future.

Should I stay or should I go? This is a question that every person asks many times throughout their lives. Should I stay in this relationship? Should I leave my home to go to school abroad? Should I take that new job? Is it time to change careers?

Living in Japan for five years, I was often asked the "should I stay or should I go" question by clients who were contemplating whether or not it was time for them to leave Japan. Some foreigners stay in Japan for decades while some leave within a year or less. Some who stay are there because they love it. Others hate it, but remain because they don't know where else to go. Some who leave are happily reintegrated back in their country of choice. Others return home only to regret the loss of their life in Japan.

Working with each of these different people, noticing the different processes by which they arrived at their decision and watching the results of their choices, it became clear that there were some common themes involved in the decisions that turned out well. While there is no one-size-fits-all strategy for making these types of big life decisions, the following principles have helped many clients, friends and colleagues over the last several decades to find a path that worked for them.

Read the Writing on the Wall

If you are ready to leave something or someone, you'll notice that your days are filled with constant annoyance, frustration and impatience with people and things related to your current circumstance. There may have been a time when the things that now annoy you were a constant source of wonder and excitement, and it can feel confusing to not know when or why things changed.

It is natural to experience some frustration in any situation or relationship, but if it has become a significant part of each day, heed the warning bells. Do you fantasize regularly about the next time you can leave the country? Do you no longer get excited about going to work each day? Do you find yourself with no interest in planning fun things to do with your spouse? All of these signal that a change may be in order.

Know What You Are Leaving — the Good and the Bad

Many people leave a situation prematurely because they let their frustrations overwhelm them. Some of my friends returned home from Japan to find that the stress lifted once they were out of the pressure cooker of life in a foreign country. From this point, they were able to see that the great things about their life in Japan outnumbered the negatives and longed to return. Some did return to great success. Others did only to have their frustrations overtake them once again.

If frustrations in some area of your life are overwhelming you and you are getting ready to call it quits, take some time to think about not only the annoyances that you will be leaving behind, but also all of the good things about the situation. Look at the good and the bad as objectively as possible. Ask yourself what you might be losing by leaving and if there might not be another way to deal with your frustrations while still sticking around to enjoy all of the good things.

Pro and con lists are a simple tool to help you do this. The interesting thing about lists is that, while they seem very logical, they are actually a tool for accessing your intuition as well. The act of writing things down gets them out of your head where they have a tendency to go around in circles without reaching any conclusion. When you write down all the reasons for staying and leaving, the hope is that you come up with two lists of obviously different length. You might think that the longer list dictates the one you should choose but this is not always the case. Seeing things in black and white helps you to evaluate their relative importance. There may be only three items on your pro list for leaving your job and twelve reasons why you shouldn't, but if the three are more important for you, leaving would still make sense.

Everyone wants to feel like their choices make sense, but it is important to understand that it is your heart that makes the best choices, not your head. If you Google "decision making tools" you will come up with hundreds of great tools to help you access your logic. At the end of the day, however, logic and your heart may not be aligned. The great thing about using these tools is that they still give you the answers. If your intuition is aligned with the logical choice you will feel good about the direction dictated by the tool. If you don't feel good about the choice that your list dictates, then you still have your answer.

Know What You Are Going To

The final key to making the right decision about when to leave is to have a clear picture of what you are going to. Running away from something is less likely to have a positive outcome than running toward something. Spend some time thinking about your passions and create an ideal vision of the next phase of your life. Once you have this in mind, it might become clear that a few more months — or even years — in your current situation will help you lay the foundation for what you want to do next in your life and work. It might also make it crystal clear that your current situation is not moving you towards your ideal vision of yourself, your life or your work. Regardless of which you choose, knowing what you want will help you take action to make either option more fulfilling.

Finish As You Want to Start

If, after all of the above steps, you are still confused, it might be time to seek some help. A professional counselor or coach can be invaluable in helping you to get clarity on what you really want or to deal with the underlying fears that are keeping you locked in indecision. If looking at pros, cons, consequences, worst-case scenarios and other methods of analyzing a decision is not working, there is a good chance that there is something you still need to learn from the situation you are in before you move on. This is where a principle I call "finish as you want to start" comes in.

This principle evolved out of what I perceived, in my younger years, to be indecisiveness or simply the inability to let go and move on. After years of experience with myself and others I have come to realize that it is actually based in a natural need to grow from every experience. Each life circumstance you find yourself in has something to teach you. If you haven't learned that lesson, it will feel more difficult to move on because, at some level, you will feel incomplete.

I have also come to understand that the energy that we leave a situation with is brought with us to the next one. So, for example, if you leave a job from a place of feeling like a victim, there is a good chance that you will attract a new job that leaves you feeling the same. If you leave a relationship feeling taken for granted, you risk bringing this same energy into your next relationship.

A caution here: you can stay stuck in an unhealthy situation far too long by continuing to see yourself as the problem and trying to change yourself. That is not what this principle is about.

To apply this principle you need to come from a place of assuming that it is indeed time to go. From that place, ask yourself what energy you want to bring to your next job, relationship or living arrangement. Then ask yourself what you would need to do in your current situation to complete it in a way that would create more of that desired energy.

One client, for example, was ready to leave her high-level management job because she was feeling unappreciated. The reality was that the executives who were her supervisors were much less capable than she was and they couldn't grasp the full extent of the contribution she made. It also meant that they were unable to mentor her. This clarity helped her to understand that she needed to leave because she was frustrated at having to mentor others, but having no one to support her to learn and grow as well. She could have just left, but decided to put off her departure for almost a year to work towards helping her team win a major internal quality award. She wanted to leave on a high note of feeling appreciated and recognized for her efforts, so her next job would start with that energy within herself and build more of it.

There is no one method of decision-making that is right for everyone. While asking for advice can be useful, it can also be confusing. The values, principles and preferences that one person bases their decisions on may not work for someone else. The best choices are a combination of logic and instinct. Regardless of the choice you make, however, all choices require the courage and confidence to do one thing after the decision has been made: *act!*

It is natural to fear action in these moments, because action means the end of something that has been a big part of your life. Remember, however, that endings serve a function. They are the process by which we let go of the past and pave the way for a brighter future. Rather than resisting endings, learn to navigate them more skillfully, ensuring that the links you forge between past and present are built to bring forward the best of who you are.

Thank you for reading
Wabi Sabi Wisdom!

If you liked Wabi-Sabi Wisdom, we would greatly appreciate you taking a few moments to leave a review on Amazon or Goodreads.

If you send us a copy of your review, we'll send you an advanced reader copy of our next book, due out later this year. Visit: **KyoseiCoaching.com/wsw-arc/** to learn more.

For information on our training and coaching programs to support you in living an authentic life, finding authentic work, or being a conscious entrepreneur visit **KyoseiCoaching.com**

For information on our core speaking and training programs to develop authentic leadership, build a healthy workplace culture, foster work-life balance, engage your employees, and transform your workplace, visit **KyoseiConsulting.com**

The Life-Work Integrity™ Coaching Program

Whether you are a leader, entrepreneur, employee, stay-at-home-parent, or anywhere in between, the Life-Work Integrity Coaching Program is designed to help you "shift the balance" to greater energy, purpose, passion, well-being and performance. You will discover the forces that drive and block vitality, fulfillment and results and learn strategies to thrive — permanently — in life and work.

Clients go through the Life-Work Integrity™ Coaching program for many different reasons. These reasons are as unique as each individual, however here are some common results:

- Enhanced energy, balance and wellbeing;
- Improved productivity and performance;
- Increased career clarity, alignment and success;
- Mid and late career re-engagement;
- Reduced stress;
- Increased leadership and business results; and
- Stronger foundations for personal and business sustainability.

Ideal candidates include:

- Employees or entrepreneurs struggling with stress, burnout, wellness, or life-work balance;
- Peak performers who want to raise the bar on their energy, performance, fulfillment and health; and
- Anyone who is passionate about taking the lead in transforming their work or their workplace by building a stronger personal foundation of authenticity, alignment and integrity for themselves.

Note: This program is also available in workshop format for teams, or as a certification program for leaders who wish to build their skill set to enhance performance, well-being and engagement in their employees.

For more information, to sign up for our newsletter, or to get some great free resources on living an authentic life, visit **KyoseiCoaching.com**.

About Kyosei Consulting

Kyosei Consulting is a leadership development and training company that helps people at all levels of an organization to take the lead in transforming their work and their workplaces for the better. Here are a few of our most popular speaking topics and training programs:

- **The Mindsets of Workplace Transformation:** discover and bust the beliefs that get in the way of building high-performance, high-fulfillment cultures
- **Engage Your Team:** inspire passion, purpose and performance at work
- **Engage Yourself:** take the lead on career alignment and personal fulfillment at work
- **Beyond Balance:** build foundations to thrive in life and work

For more information visit **KyoseiConsulting.com**, or e-mail us at **info@KyoseiConsulting.com** with details of your conference or event, your objectives and your budget and we will be in touch to discuss which of our programs would best suit your needs.

About the Author

Andrea Jacques is a dynamic speaker, trainer, coach and thought leader in the field of workplace transformation, employee engagement, and purpose-driven work. As the founder of Kyosei Consulting International, she has more than two decades of experience working with companies worldwide to create high-performance, high-fulfillment cultures. Andrea began her career in work and workplace transformation with academic, government and health care institutions in Canada, but honed her "east-meets-west" approach during 5 years working in Japan with corporations like Chase Manhattan, Disney, Fuji, NEC and the Center for International Communication and Management. Based in Vancouver, Canada, Andrea is deeply passionate about working with companies of all sizes to re-imagine work, workplaces, and the nature of business to create a world where everyone thrives.

35490134R10128